PLACE VALUE

math workbook

Grade 4

D1737498

This book belongs to:

Learning Lab

I hope your child benefits from this book.

I am a small independent publisher and love creating books just like this. It would mean the world to me if you could spend just a minute to leave a review on Amazon. It would really help a lot.

Please scan below and leave your review.

A Note to Parents and Teachers

Place Value Math Workbook For Grade 4 aims to serve as a mathematics companion for Forth Graders and pupils usually between ages 9 to 10. It is suitable for pupils who self-study at home to supplement their school work, or those who are home schooled.

It is dedicated to assist pupils to revise and practise Place Value sub-topics in an effective and efficient way, and also to help them gain confidence in handling the questions in this topic. Being a fundamental topic, a good understanding is essential in laying a good foundation in Mathematics.

It contains the following features:
- Date and Score board at the top of each page to track the progress of the pupils
- Comprehensive Notes and Worked Examples in which concepts are emphasized. These worked examples will help them learn to solve similar types of questions.
- Solutions are provided for every first question in the sections, and also guidance for the first few questions for the more challenging sections.

Answers are provided at the back of the book according to page numbers, for self-revision and self-correction.

Dylah Othman
Learning Lab

Table of Contents

Whole Number Place Value

Base Ten Blocks

Place value refers to the value that each digit in a number has, based on its position.

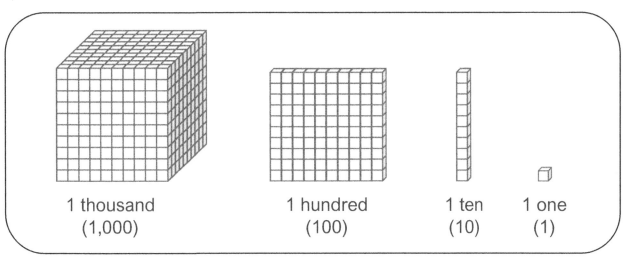

| 1 thousand (1,000) | 1 hundred (100) | 1 ten (10) | 1 one (1) |

For the number 1, 462:

Thousands	Hundreds	Tens	Ones
1	4	6	2

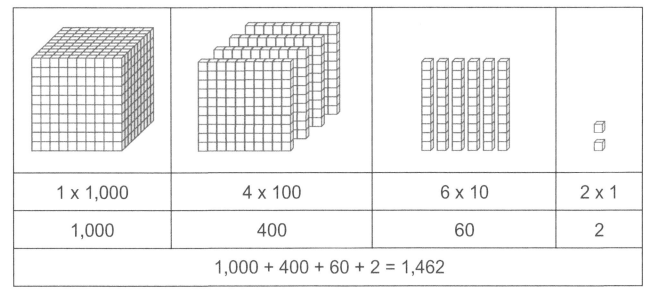

1 x 1,000	4 x 100	6 x 10	2 x 1
1,000	400	60	2
1,000 + 400 + 60 + 2 = 1,462			

The 1 is in the thousands place, 4 is in the hundreds place, the 6 is in the tens place, and the 2 is in the ones place.

Score | / |

Date: _____

Find the number that the base ten blocks are showing.

1)
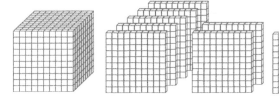

| 1 | thousand | 7 | hundreds |
| 2 | tens | 4 | ones |

= | 1,000 + 700 + 20 + 4 |

= | 1,724 |

2)
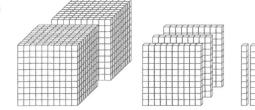

| | thousands | | hundreds |
| | tens | | ones |

= | |

= | |

3)
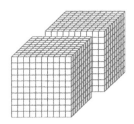

| | thousands | | hundreds |
| | tens | | ones |

= | |

= | |

4)
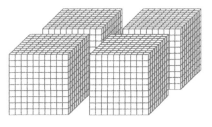

| | thousands | | hundreds |
| | tens | | ones |

= | |

= | |

Find the number that the base ten blocks are showing.

1)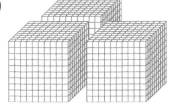

[ ] thousands   [ ] hundreds

[ ] tens   [ ] ones

= [   ]

= [   ]

2)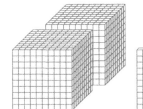

[ ] thousand   [ ] hundreds

[ ] tens   [ ] ones

= [   ]

= [   ]

3)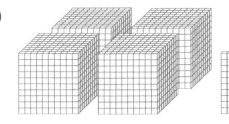

[ ] thousand   [ ] hundreds

[ ] tens   [ ] ones

= [   ]

= [   ]

4)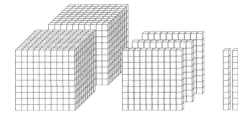

[ ] thousand   [ ] hundreds

[ ] tens   [ ] ones

= [   ]

= [   ]

Score /

Date: _____

Find the number that the base ten blocks are showing.

1)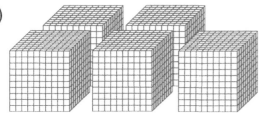

☐ thousands   ☐ hundreds

☐ tens   ☐ ones

= ☐

= ☐

2)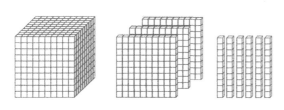

☐ thousands   ☐ hundreds

☐ tens   ☐ ones

= ☐

= ☐

3)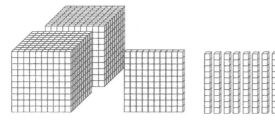

☐ thousands   ☐ hundreds

☐ tens   ☐ ones

= ☐

= ☐

4)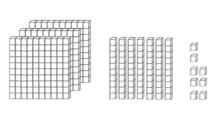

☐ thousand   ☐ hundreds

☐ tens   ☐ ones

= ☐

= ☐

Date: _____   **Score** | / |

Find the number that the base ten blocks are showing.

1)

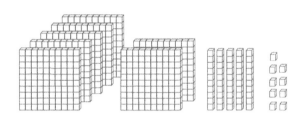

| | thousands | | hundreds |
| | tens | | ones |

= [   ]

= [   ]

2)

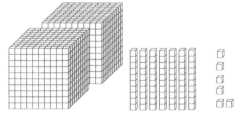

| | thousands | | hundreds |
| | tens | | ones |

= [   ]

= [   ]

3)

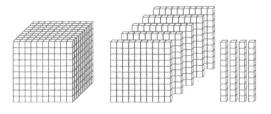

| | thousands | | hundreds |
| | tens | | ones |

= [   ]

= [   ]

4)

| | thousand | | hundreds |
| | tens | | ones |

= [   ]

= [   ]

Score [/]

Standard and Expanded Forms

Thousands Period			Ones Period		
Hundred Thousands	Ten Thousands	Thousands	Hundreds	Tens	Ones
100,000	10,000	1,000	100	10	1
2	7	3	0	1	4

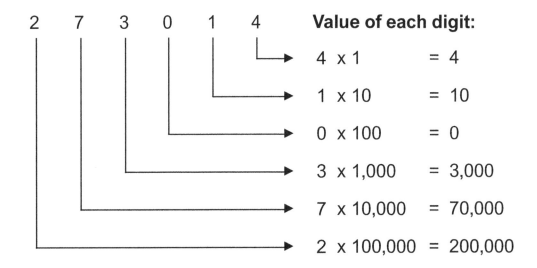

Value of each digit:

4 x 1	=	4
1 x 10	=	10
0 x 100	=	0
3 x 1,000	=	3,000
7 x 10,000	=	70,000
2 x 100,000	=	200,000

Standard Form	273,014 (or 273 014 without comma)
Expanded Form	200,000 + 70,000 + 3,000 + 10 + 4
	2 hundred thousands + 7 ten thousands + 3 thousands + 1 ten + 4 ones

Largest and Smallest Digits

The <u>largest</u> digit in a number is the one furthest to the left, digit 2 in the above example. The <u>smallest</u> digit in any number will always be the ones place.

Thousands Period			Ones Period		
Hundred Thousands	Ten Thousands	Thousands	Hundreds	Tens	Ones
100,000	10,000	1,000	100	10	1
2	7	3	0	1	4

two hundred seventy-three thousand   *fourteen*

Written (Word) Form	Two hundred seventy-three thousand, fourteen or Two hundred and seventy-three, and twenty-four (with 'and')

Digit Zero

The place value of digit 0 in a number is always zero because when multiplied by any number, result is always 0. It is used as a placeholder to show an empty place value. In the above example, since the digit is 0 for place value hundreds, the value for hundreds is 0 (zero).

When writing numbers in written (or word) form, if a digit is zero in a place value, we exclude them in the expression, just like in expanded form.

Score   /

Date: _____

Fill in the place value chart below.

		Thousands			Ones		
		Hundred Thousands	Ten Thousands	Thousands	Hundreds	Tens	Ones
1)	146,309	1	4	6	3	0	9
2)	27,820						
3)	6,124						
4)	53,476						
5)	231						
6)	122,917						
7)	495,234						
8)	76,085						
9)	321,498						
10)	14,372						

Write each number in expanded form.

1)	146,309	*100,000 + 40,000 + 6,000 + 300 + 9*
2)	27,820	
3)	6,124	
4)	53,476	
5)	231	
6)	122,917	
7)	495,234	
8)	76,085	
9)	321,498	
10)	14,372	

Score ____ / ____

Date: _____

Fill in the place value chart below.

	Thousands			Ones		
	Hundred Thousands	Ten Thousands	Thousands	Hundreds	Tens	Ones
1) 712,897						
2) 30,204						
3) 2,560						
4) 843,629						
5) 48,715						
6) 942						
7) 6,298						
8) 523,624						
9) 69,132						
10) 951,487						

Write each number in expanded form.

1)	712,897	
2)	30,204	
3)	2,560	
4)	843,629	
5)	48,715	
6)	942	
7)	6,298	
8)	523,624	
9)	69,132	
10)	951,487	

Score /

Date: ____________

Fill in the place value chart below.

		Thousands			Ones		
		Hundred Thousands	Ten Thousands	Thousands	Hundreds	Tens	Ones
1)	852						
2)	671,432						
3)	30,876						
4)	274,980						
5)	72,681						
6)	9,234						
7)	378						
8)	236,912						
9)	432,689						
10)	645,001						

Write each number in expanded form.

1)	852	
2)	671,432	
3)	30,876	
4)	274,980	
5)	72,681	
6)	9,234	
7)	378	
8)	236,912	
9)	432,689	
10)	645,001	

Score   /   Date: _____

Fill in the place value chart below.

		Thousands			Ones		
		Hundred Thousands	Ten Thousands	Thousands	Hundreds	Tens	Ones
1)	81,930						
2)	935						
3)	241,009						
4)	6,827						
5)	78,033						
6)	104,058						
7)	63,981						
8)	690						
9)	500,834						
10)	1,008						

Write each number in expanded form.

1)	81,930	
2)	935	
3)	241,009	
4)	6,827	
5)	78,033	
6)	104,058	
7)	63,981	
8)	690	
9)	500,834	
10)	1,008	

Score   /   Date: _____

Value of Digits

Write the value of the digit 4.

1)	634,187	*4,000*
2)	17,942	
3)	481,273	
4)	795,412	
5)	172,564	

Write the value of the digit 1.

6)	634,187	
7)	17,942	
8)	481,273	
9)	795,412	
10)	172,564	

Write the value of the digit 7.

11)	634,187	
12)	17,942	
13)	481,273	
14)	795,412	
15)	172,564	

Write the value of the digit 9.

1)	423,8**9**1	
2)	2**9**8,135	
3)	62,**9**08	
4)	82**9**,602	
5)	**9**46,283	

Write the value of the digit 8.

6)	423,**8**91	
7)	29**8**,135	
8)	62,90**8**	
9)	**8**29,602	
10)	946,2**8**3	

Write the value of the digit 2.

11)	4**2**3,891	
12)	**2**98,135	
13)	6**2**,908	
14)	819,60**2**	
15)	946,**2**83	

Score | /

Date: _____

Write the value of the digit 5.

1)	360,9**5**1	
2)	**5**,638	
3)	**5**03,967	
4)	629,**5**13	
5)	1**5**6,380	

Write the value of the digit 3.

6)	**3**60,951	
7)	75,6**3**8	
8)	50**3**,967	
9)	629,51**3**	
10)	156,**3**80	

Write the value of the digit 6.

11)	3**6**0,951	
12)	75,**6**38	
13)	503,9**6**7	
14)	**6**29,513	
15)	15**6**,380	

Write the value of the digit 9.

1)	724,**9**31	
2)	48,75**9**	
3)	**9**70,423	
4)	45**9**,270	
5)	6**9**7,048	

Write the value of the digit 4.

6)	72**4**,931	
7)	**4**8,759	
8)	970,**4**23	
9)	**4**59,270	
10)	697,0**4**8	

Write the value of the digit 7.

11)	**7**24,931	
12)	48,**7**59	
13)	9**7**0,423	
14)	459,2**7**0	
15)	697,048	

Score | /

Date: _____

Fill in the blanks.

1) $800,000 + 50,000 + 2,000 + 300 + 70 + 9 =$ ⬚

2) $500,000 + 90,000 + 400 +$ ⬚ $+ 8 = 590,498$

3) $700,000 + 50,000 + 7,000 +$ ⬚ $+ 40 = 757,940$

4) $300,000 +$ ⬚ $+ 2,000 + 600 + 50 + 1 = 302,651$

5) $50,000 + 7,000 + 200 +$ ⬚ $+ 9 = 57,269$

6)   ⬚ $+ 70,000 + 8,000 + 400 + 70 = 378,470$

7) $200,734 =$ ⬚ $+ 700 + 30 + 4$

8) $40,000 + 5,000 + 600 + 80 + 4 =$ ⬚

9) $156,002 = 100,000 + 50,000 +$ ⬚ $+ 2$

10) $18,931 = 10,000 + 8,000 +$ ⬚ $+ 30 + 1$

11)   ⬚ $+ 5,000 + 600 + 70 + 4 = 25,674$

12) $503,862 = 500,000 +$ ⬚ $+ 800 + 60 + 2$

13) $200,000 + 7,000 + 500 + 60 =$ ⬚

14) $10,000 + 5,000 +$ ⬚ $+ 8 = 15,058$

15) $90,470 = 90,000 +$ ⬚ $+ 70$

Fill in the blanks.

1)   200,000 + 30,000 + 400 + 60 + 8 = [   ]

2)   963,250 = 900,000 + [   ] + 3,000 + 200 + 50

3)   [   ] = 700,000 + 40,000 + 8,000 + 200 + 30 + 5

4)   600,000 + 90,000 + [   ] + 500 + 80 + 2 = 693,582

5)   500,000 + [   ] + 5,000 + 100 + 40 + 6 = 575,146

6)   [   ] = 200,000 + 700 + 20 + 1

7)   300,000 + [   ] + 7,000 + 500 + 10 + 2 = 307,512

8)   20,000 + 5,000 + [   ] + 40 + 6 = 25,746

9)   106,452 = 100,000 + [   ] + 400 + 50 + 2

10)   500,032 = [   ] + 30 + 2

11)   400,000 + 80,000 + 1,000 + 400 + 3 = [   ]

12)   [   ] + 4,000 + 500 + 60 + 2 = 204,562

13)   300,000 + [   ] + 5,000 + 100 + 8 = 325,108

14)   400,000 + 80,000 + [   ] + 50 + 8 = 480,258

15)   [   ] = 10,000 + 6,000 + 700 + 30

Score   *I*   Date: _____

Fill in the blanks.

1) $20,000 +$ ⬜ $+ 700 + 30 + 5 = 26,735$

2) $679,004 = 600,000 + 70,000 +$ ⬜ $+ 4$

3)   ⬜ $+ 3,000 + 200 + 60 + 8 = 403,268$

4) $200,000 + 20,000 + 300 + 80 + 9 =$ ⬜

5) $700,000 +$ ⬜ $+ 4,000 + 200 + 90 + 3 = 724,293$

6)   ⬜ $+ 500 + 20 + 7 = 400,527$

7) $106,902 =$ ⬜ $+ 6,000 + 900 + 2$

8) $50,000 + 3,000 + 400 + 20 =$ ⬜

9) $900,000 + 10,000 +$ ⬜ $+ 200 + 50 + 8 = 913,258$

10) $403,102 =$ ⬜ $+ 3,000 + 100 + 2$

11) $50,000 + 8,000 + 3 =$ ⬜

12) $900,000 +$ ⬜ $+ 5,000 + 100 + 40 + 7 = 955,147$

13) $20,000 +$ ⬜ $+ 400 + 80 + 1 = 23,481$

14) $300,000 + 70,000 +$ ⬜ $+ 600 + 30 + 8 = 372,638$

15)   ⬜ $+ 30,000 + 4,000 + 600 + 10 + 1 = 834,611$

Date: _____

Score | / |

Written Forms

Write in numerals.

1)	Thirty-five thousand, seven hundred twelve	*35,712*
2)	Two hundred fifty-six thousand, two hundred seventy-two	
3)	Forty-nine thousand, six hundred thirty-one	
4)	Seven hundred sixty-one thousand, two hundred fifty-five	
5)	Three hundred twenty-nine thousand, two hundred fifty-six	
6)	Three hundred thirteen thousand, nine hundred	
7)	Five hundred eleven thousand, two hundred eight	
8)	Twenty-three thousand, seven hundred thirty-one	
9)	Four hundred thirty thousand, nine hundred sixty-two	
10)	Seventy-one thousand, two hundred seven	
11)	Twelve thousand, four hundred ninety-five	
12)	Eight hundred fifty-three	
13)	One hundred forty-five thousand, three hundred one	
14)	Nine thousand, two hundred ninety-nine	
15)	Fifty-eight thousand, two hundred sixty-four	

Score   /

Date: _____

Write in numerals.

1)	Two hundred fifty-eight thousand, six hundred forty-five	
2)	One hundred fourteen thousand, twelve	
3)	Six hundred one thousand, two hundred fifty-four	
4)	Three hundred thousand, four hundred eighty-five	
5)	Five thousand, six hundred seventy-two	
6)	Nine hundred thirteen thousand, forty-nine	
7)	Eighty-two thousand, four hundred thirty-one	
8)	Five hundred nine thousand, two hundred twenty-four	
9)	Two hundred seventy-four thousand, one hundred fifty-eight	
10)	Four hundred twelve thousand	
11)	Nine thousand, three hundred sixty-five	
12)	Three hundred five thousand, two hundred forty-one	
13)	Six hundred fifteen thousand, nine hundred six	
14)	Eighty thousand, five hundred twenty-two	
15)	Seven hundred forty-three thousand, five hundred sixteen	

Write in numerals.

1)	Twenty-six thousand, four hundred sixty-eight	
2)	Nine hundred five thousand, eighty-nine	
3)	Sixty-four thousand, seven hundred twelve	
4)	Three hundred forty-five thousand, two hundred three	
5)	Five hundred thousand, two hundred sixty-one	
6)	Eight hundred sixteen thousand, one hundred ninety-two	
7)	Six hundred seven thousand, five hundred forty	
8)	Two hundred ninety thousand, four hundred eight	
9)	Thirty-six thousand, three hundred fifty-nine	
10)	Eight hundred thirty-five thousand, two hundred sixteen	
11)	Twenty-seven thousand, nine hundred twenty-three	
12)	Ninety-one thousand, two hundred forty-six	
13)	Eleven thousand, three hundred fifty	
14)	Two hundred forty-three thousand, seven	
15)	Five thousand, three hundred ninety-one	

Score   /   Date: _____

Write in numerals.

1)	Four hundred eighteen thousand, three hundred two	
2)	Two hundred fifty thousand, six hundred eleven	
3)	Seven hundred sixty-one thousand, four hundred seventy-five	
4)	One hundred thousand, eighty-two	
5)	Ninety-eight thousand, four hundred thirty-one	
6)	Seven thousand, two hundred fifteen	
7)	Four hundred twenty thousand, three hundred ninety-nine	
8)	Three hundred two thousand, one hundred eight	
9)	Twelve thousand, four hundred sixty-three	
10)	One hundred eighteen thousand, one hundred ninety-two	
11)	Five thousand, two hundred twenty-five	
12)	One hundred seventy four thousand, three hundred sixty-two	
13)	Ninety-five thousand, three hundred twenty-eight	
14)	Six hundred thirty-one thousand, two hundred eighty	
15)	Four hundred nine thousand, thirty-nine	

Write in words.

1)	531,912	*Five hundred thirty-one thousand, nine hundred twelve*
2)	259,720	
3)	86,674	
4)	9,603	
5)	14,827	
6)	630,067	
7)	486,175	
8)	5,609	
9)	375,005	
10)	804,300	
11)	27,095	
12)	6,320	

Score | / |

Date: _____

Write in words.

1)	73,765	
2)	2,695	
3)	900,127	
4)	18,956	
5)	350	
6)	349,235	
7)	58,007	
8)	237,485	
9)	109,033	
10)	2,156	
11)	86,579	
12)	925,834	

Write in words.

1)	3,802	
2)	83,389	
3)	590,153	
4)	600,346	
5)	27,105	
6)	230,400	
7)	789,034	
8)	172,982	
9)	907,234	
10)	533	
11)	81,290	
12)	415,011	

Score | / |

Date: _____

Write in words.

1)	76,982	
2)	103,983	
3)	51,008	
4)	431	
5)	58,992	
6)	418,900	
7)	283,488	
8)	67,093	
9)	2,782	
10)	120,000	
11)	83,320	
12)	739	

Use place value to write these numbers in 2 other forms.

1)

Standard form	
Word form	
Expanded form	200,000 + 50,000 + 6,000 + 70 + 8

2)

Standard form	61,785
Word form	
Expanded form	

3)

Standard form	
Word form	Four hundred thirty-seven thousand, six hundred twenty-nine
Expanded form	

4)

Standard form	
Word form	Ninety-eight thousand, seven hundred fifty-seven
Expanded form	

5)

Standard form	
Word form	
Expanded form	800,000 + 80,000 + 6,000 + 900 + 20 + 7

Score /   Date: _____

Use place value to write these numbers in 2 other forms.

1)

Standard form	
Word form	Seventy thousand, nine hundred thirty-five
Expanded form	

2)

Standard form	
Word form	
Expanded form	800,000 + 50,000 + 1,000 + 700 + 30 + 2

3)

Standard form	
Word form	Five hundred thirty-eight thousand, two hundred five
Expanded form	

4)

Standard form	95,392
Word form	
Expanded form	

5)

Standard form	
Word form	
Expanded form	700,000 + 40,000 + 300 + 60 + 8

Use place value to write these numbers in 2 other forms.

1)

Standard form	
Word form	Two hundred fifty-one thousand, eight hundred twelve
Expanded form	

2)

Standard form	133,690
Word form	
Expanded form	

3)

Standard form	
Word form	Six hundred eighty-five thousand, nine hundred thirty-two
Expanded form	

4)

Standard form	
Word form	
Expanded form	40,000 + 6,000 + 500 + 30 + 9

5)

Standard form	306,560
Word form	
Expanded form	

Place Values Relationships

Moving to the Left One Place

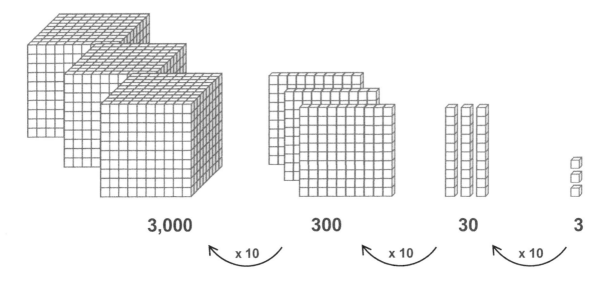

Thousands			Ones		
Hundred Thousands	Ten Thousands	Thousands	Hundreds	Tens	Ones
100,000	10,000	1,000	100	10	1
300,000	30,000	3,000	300	30	3

The digit 3 shifts 1 place to the left when we multiply by 10. Its value becomes 10 times more:

- value of 3 tens is 10 times the value of 3 ones
- value of 3 hundreds is 10 times the value of 3 tens
- value of 3 thousands is 10 times the value of 3 hundreds
- value of 30 thousands is 10 times the value of 3 thousands
- value of 300 thousands is 10 times the value of 30 thousands

10 times more means we add 1 zero to the right of that number

10 times more

Place Value	
400	40

10 times lesser

The value of 4 in 400 is 10 times more the value of 4 in 40.
The value of 4 in 400 is 10 times bigger than the value of 4 in 40.
The value of 4 in 40 is 10 times lesser than the value of 4 in 400.

Place Value	
8,405	742

The value of 4 in 8,405 is 10 times the value of 4 in 742.
The value of 4 in 8,405 is 10 times bigger than the value of 4 in 742.
The value of 4 in 742 is 10 times lesser than the value of 4 in 8,405.

When a digit shifts 1 place value to the left, its value becomes 10 times more. It becomes 10 times lesser when it shifts 1 place value to the right.

100 times more

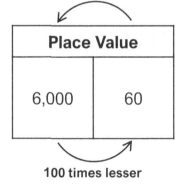

Place Value	
6,000	60

100 times lesser

The value of 6 in 6,000 is 100 times the value of 6 in 60.
The value of 6 in 6,000 is 100 times bigger than the value of 6 in 60.
The value of 6 in 60 is 100 times lesser than the value of 6 in 6,000.

Place Value	
26,982	15,168

The value of 6 in 26,982 is 100 times the value of 6 in 15,168.
The value of 6 in 26,982 is 100 times bigger than the value of 6 in 15,168.
The value of 6 in 15,168 is 100 times lesser than the value of 6 in 26,982.

When a digit shifts 2 place values to the left, its value becomes 100 times more. It becomes 100 times lesser when it shifts 2 place values to the right.

Score   /

Date: _____

Compare the values of the underlined digits.

1)

93,4̲25	124,7̲62

The value of 4 in ___124,762___ is __10__ times the value of 4 in

___93,425___.

2)

837,6̲05	6̲,291

The value of 6 in _____ is _____ times the value of 6 in

_____.

3)

25̲,002	682,35̲4

The value of 5 in _____ is _____ times the value of 5 in

_____.

4)

591,08̲3	8̲,403

The value of 8 in _____ is _____ times the value of 8 in

_____.

5)

461̲,735	920,31̲6

The value of 1 in _____ is _____ times the value of 1 in

_____.

6)

503̲,721	23̲6,804

The value of 3 in _____ is _____ times the value of 3 in

_____.

Compare the values of the underlined digits.

1)

<u>6</u>0,934	57<u>6</u>,204

The value of 6 in _____ is _____ times the value of 6 in

_____.

2)

91,<u>4</u>75	7<u>4</u>1

The value of 4 in _____ is _____ times the value of 4 in

_____.

3)

9<u>8</u>,957	421,<u>8</u>93

The value of 8 in _____ is _____ times the value of 8 in

_____.

4)

293,6<u>7</u>1	9<u>7</u>,623

The value of 7 in _____ is _____ times the value of 7 in

_____.

5)

<u>5</u>7,249	183,<u>5</u>92

The value of 5 in _____ is _____ times the value of 5 in

_____.

6)

40<u>3</u>,721	2<u>3</u>6,804

The value of 3 in _____ is _____ times the value of 3 in

_____.

Score   /   Date: _____

Compare the values of the underlined digits.

1)

| 193,7<u>3</u>2 | 86,5<u>7</u>4 |

The value of 7 in _____ is _____ times the value of 7 in

_____.

2)

| 295,<u>3</u>71 | 18<u>3</u>,004 |

The value of 3 in _____ is _____ times the value of 3 in

_____.

3)

| 8,63<u>2</u> | 5<u>2</u>,734 |

The value of 2 in _____ is _____ times the value of 2 in

_____.

4)

| 733,<u>5</u>98 | 12<u>5</u>,867 |

The value of 5 in _____ is _____ times the value of 5 in

_____.

5)

| 4<u>9</u>,627 | <u>9</u>28,645 |

The value of 9 in _____ is _____ times the value of 9 in

_____.

6)

| 72,9<u>3</u>0 | 19<u>3</u>,224 |

The value of 3 in _____ is _____ times the value of 3 in

_____.

1) Circle the number having place value of 3 that is 10 times more than 3 ones.

| a) 3,812 | b) 138 | c) 2,351 |

2) Circle the number having place value of 6 that is 10 times lesser than 6 thousands.

| a) 260,971 | b) 7,692 | c) 692,381 |

3) Circle the number having place value of 2 that is 10 times lesser than 2 hundreds.

| a) 5,023 | b) 9,209 | c) 2,941 |

4) Circle the number having place value of 7 that is 10 times more than 7 ten thousands.

| a) 762,081 | b) 197,055 | c) 70,612 |

5) Circle the number having place value of 8 that is 100 times more than 8 tens.

| a) 589,371 | b) 60,825 | c) 218,936 |

6) Circle the number having place value of 5 that is 10 times lesser than 5 tens.

| a) 25,074 | b) 69,518 | c) 180,345 |

7) Circle the number having place value of 1 that is 100 times more than 1 one.

| a) 12 | b) 7,150 | c) 612,034 |

8) Circle the number having place value of 4 that is 100 times lesser than 4 hundreds.

| a) 34,067 | b) 491,082 | c) 6,134 |

Score   /   Date: _____

1) Circle the number having place value of 9 that is 10 times more than 9 ten thousands.

| a) 892,620 | b) 976,025 | c) 569,172 |

2) Circle the number having place value of 5 that is 100 times more than 5 tens.

| a) 71,352 | b) 865 | c) 15,483 |

3) Circle the number having place value of 3 that is 10 times lesser than 3 hundreds.

| a) 83,921 | b) 24,632 | c)12,399 |

4) Circle the number having place value of 4 that is 10 times more than 4 thousands.

| a) 49,312 | b) 684,035 | c) 456,791 |

5) Circle the number having place value of 2 that is 100 times more than 2 hundreds.

| a) 82,403 | b) 720,519 | c) 51,205 |

6) Circle the number having place value of 7 that is 10 times lesser than 7 hundreds.

| a) 6,387 | b) 92,573 | c) 157,392 |

7) Circle the number having place value of 6 that is 10 times more than 6 tens.

| a) 9,265 | b) 13,687 | c) 62,823 |

8) Circle the number having place value of 9 that is 100 times lesser than 9 hundreds.

| a) 95,381 | b) 81,759 | c) 9,742 |

1) Circle the number having place value of 8 that is 100 times more than 8 ones.

| a) 8,932 | b) 183 | c) 47,851 |

2) Circle the number having place value of 2 that is 10 times more than 2 thousands.

| a) 69,281 | b) 428,095 | c) 230,794 |

3) Circle the number having place value of 7 that is 10 times lesser than 7 hundreds.

| a) 17,035 | b) 901,782 | c) 2,476 |

4) Circle the number having place value of 6 that is 10 times more than 6 ten thousands.

| a) 56,903 | b) 39,217 | c) 625,102 |

5) Circle the number having place value of 3 that is 100 times more than 3 ones.

| a) 7,438 | b) 9,325 | c) 21,864 |

6) Circle the number having place value of 4 that is 100 times lesser than 4 hundreds.

| a) 234,120 | b) 36,418 | c) 564 |

7) Circle the number having place value of 9 that is 10 times more than 9 ten thousands.

| a) 936,804 | b) 713,945 | c) 269,735 |

8) Circle the number having place value of 5 that is 10 times lesser than 5 thousands.

| a) 54,812 | b) 8,529 | c) 15,306 |

Score [/]   Date: _____

Comparing and Ordering Numbers

Comparing Numbers

When given 2 numbers, we can compare them.

Step 1:   Stack the 2 numbers, one on top of the other, making sure the place values of both numbers are aligned

Step 2:   Start comparing from the far left, the digits having the largest place value; continue comparing each place value until we find the difference

Hundred Thousands
Ten Thousands
Thousands
Hundreds
Tens
Ones

153,610
152,691

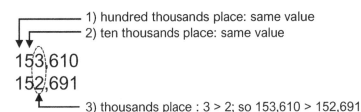

1) hundred thousands place: same value
2) ten thousands place: same value

153,610
152,691

3) thousands place : 3 > 2; so 153,610 > 152,691

$$153{,}610 \;(>)\; 152{,}691$$

Use < or > to compare the numbers.

1)   324,120 $(>)$ 320,123

2)   83,293 $(\bigcirc)$ 8,932

3)   7,592 $(\bigcirc)$ 7,955

4)   29,744 $(\bigcirc)$ 92,744

5)   4,803 $(\bigcirc)$ 4,830

6)   126,300 $(\bigcirc)$ 261,100

7)   20,104 $(\bigcirc)$ 20,140

8)   97,675 $(\bigcirc)$ 97,660

9)   52,192 $(\bigcirc)$ 59,219

10)   459,721 $(\bigcirc)$ 954,721

11)   600,281 $(\bigcirc)$ 602,180

12)   7,923 $(\bigcirc)$ 7,239

13)   945 $(\bigcirc)$ 549

14)   50,456 $(\bigcirc)$ 5,045

Use < or > to compare the numbers.

1)   51,893 ◯ 15,893

2)   614,902 ◯ 604,902

3)   79,101 ◯ 9,710

4)   332,012 ◯ 333,012

5)   471,009 ◯ 471,900

6)   672 ◯ 827

7)   37,801 ◯ 37,081

8)   182,390 ◯ 108,390

9)   700,230 ◯ 790,230

10)   582,632 ◯ 682,632

11)   287,102 ◯ 287,201

12)   347,932 ◯ 347,792

13)   491,567 ◯ 419,867

14)   98,782 ◯ 98,820

15)   619,312 ◯ 619,213

16)   109,892 ◯ 901,289

17)   337,921 ◯ 373,921

18)   723,152 ◯ 720,152

19)   86,677 ◯ 80,671

20)   532,800 ◯ 530,900

21)   493,925 ◯ 493,952

22)   62,980 ◯ 63,100

23)   861,700 ◯ 867,100

24)   18,621 ◯ 18,701

Use < or > to compare the numbers.

1) 731,020 ◯ 731,200

2) 216,555 ◯ 261,333

3) 9,241 ◯ 9,941

4) 534,689 ◯ 534,089

5) 80,342 ◯ 80,300

6) 61,932 ◯ 69,123

7) 90,651 ◯ 99,615

8) 100,956 ◯ 100,900

9) 461,570 ◯ 416,570

10) 27,003 ◯ 27,030

11) 502,909 ◯ 502,009

12) 750,670 ◯ 570,670

13) 48,204 ◯ 48,240

14) 32,472 ◯ 30,742

15) 88,562 ◯ 88,600

16) 39,201 ◯ 39,102

17) 560,921 ◯ 506,129

18) 156,002 ◯ 165,002

19) 9,461 ◯ 9,416

20) 60,341 ◯ 69,034

21) 201,833 ◯ 200,834

22) 730,158 ◯ 703,158

23) 420,736 ◯ 422,637

24) 93,489 ◯ 9,349

Use < or > to compare the numbers.

1) 88,932 ◯ 88,732 2) 562,040 ◯ 562,400

3) 20,932 ◯ 29,032 4) 724,099 ◯ 724,909

5) 162,320 ◯ 160,390 6) 36,903 ◯ 39,903

7) 133,260 ◯ 133,620 8) 54,087 ◯ 54,887

9) 281,126 ◯ 280,621 10) 69,851 ◯ 9,851

11) 341,009 ◯ 431,009 12) 222,573 ◯ 228,357

13) 160,125 ◯ 106,125 14) 73,981 ◯ 703,981

15) 20,803 ◯ 20,083 16) 489,133 ◯ 489,311

17) 801 ◯ 810 18) 60,002 ◯ 60,200

19) 5,218 ◯ 5,278 20) 39,023 ◯ 30,923

21) 40,636 ◯ 40,633 22) 821,602 ◯ 820,006

23) 9,143 ◯ 9,431 24) 79,219 ◯ 76,291

Score | / | Date: _____

Shade the largest number.

1) | 672,093 | 679,832 | 670,172 |

2) | 8,902 | 8,792 | 8,279 |

3) | 134,789 | 103,479 | 14,378 |

4) | 91,006 | 90,697 | 97,098 |

5) | 7,908 | 7,991 | 7,098 |

6) | 108 | 181 | 118 |

7) | 52,091 | 50,291 | 51,092 |

8) | 27,891 | 27,109 | 27,198 |

9) | 3,065 | 3,105 | 3,506 |

10) | 82,750 | 80,057 | 80,507 |

11) | 90,702 | 97,200 | 92,007 |

12) | 4,672 | 4,267 | 4,726 |

Shade the smallest number.

1) | 21,093 | 2,931 | 23,092 |

2) | 689 | 696 | 690 |

3) | 7,211 | 7,012 | 7,001 |

4) | 815,462 | 851,245 | 812,524 |

5) | 3,809 | 3,089 | 3,980 |

6) | 56,032 | 50,302 | 50,623 |

7) | 1,489 | 1,098 | 1,948 |

8) | 20,395 | 23,590 | 20,509 |

9) | 284 | 824 | 428 |

10) | 9,210 | 9,012 | 9,102 |

11) | 451,087 | 487,051 | 415,780 |

12) | 38,902 | 32,809 | 30,098 |

Score /   Date: _____

Shade the largest number.

1) | 792 | 729 | 709 |

2) | 48,102 | 40,821 | 42,810 |

3) | 562,008 | 500,826 | 520,268 |

4) | 93,295 | 99,059 | 95,309 |

5) | 3,452 | 3,025 | 3,254 |

6) | 296,782 | 206,987 | 290,627 |

7) | 6,921 | 6,129 | 6,219 |

8) | 4,053 | 4,503 | 4,350 |

9) | 852 | 8,025 | 8,520 |

10) | 1,872 | 1,278 | 1,728 |

11) | 7,602 | 70,026 | 7,026 |

12) | 534,073 | 507,343 | 547,034 |

Ordering Numbers

We can order whole numbers from least to greatest or from greatest to least. To order them, we also compare place value by place value just like when comparing two numbers. But with more numbers, it is best to put in a table.

Step 1: Compare the number of digits for each number. The greater the number of digits, the larger the number; the fewer the number of digits, the smaller the number

Step 2: Place the remaining numbers in a place value chart or stack up all the numbers on top of each other aligned by place value positions

Step 3: Starting at the far left which is the biggest place value position, compare the digits place value by place value; continue comparing each place values until we find the difference in the numbers

Order these numbers from least to greatest:

130,512   125,873   76,782   130,876

	Hundred Thousands	Ten Thousands	Thousands	Hundreds	Tens	Ones
a.	1	3	0	5	1	2
b.	1	②	5	8	7	3
c.		7	6	7	8	2
d.	1	3	0	8	7	6

> **1**
> Fewer number of digits than the rest. So, the least number

> **2**
> Compare the hundred thousands of (a), (b) & (d). All have the same number. Continue to compare ten thousands.

> **3**
> 2 ten thousands in (b) is the smallest. So, 125,873 is next least number.

> **4**
> Compare the thousands. (a) & (d) have the same number. Continue to compare hundreds.

> **5**
> 8 hundreds in (d) is bigger than 5 hundreds in (a). So, 130,876 is the greatest

c	b	a	d

least

___76,782___ , ___125,873___ , ___130,512___ , ___130,876___

least

Date: _____

Arrange the numbers from least to greatest.

1)

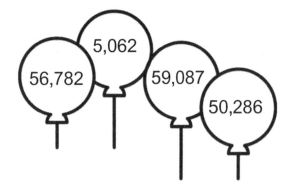

Hund. Thou.	Ten Thou.	Thou.	Hund.	Tens	Ones

_____, _____, _____, _____
least

2)

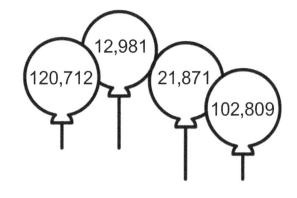

Hund. Thou.	Ten Thou.	Thou.	Hund.	Tens	Ones

_____, _____, _____, _____
least

3)

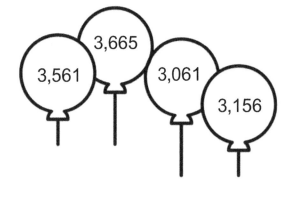

Hund. Thou.	Ten Thou.	Thou.	Hund.	Tens	Ones

_____, _____, _____, _____
least

Arrange the numbers from least to greatest.

1)

65,872	75,892	6,923	64,321

2)

218,954	123,609	137,870	210,673

3)

89,672	88,102	82,145	80,239

4)

13,843	13,047	12,004	12,426

5)

4,834	4,023	4,902	40,812

6)

313,934	331,613	33,502	306,156

7)

48,923	84,283	46,234	8,348

8)

7,894	7,462	7,012	7,264

Score /   Date: _____

Arrange the numbers from least to greatest.

1)

55,123	50,832	5,805	5,891

2)

98,672	92,903	93,001	96,734

3)

432,083	488,263	405,127	423,817

4)

2,893	21,527	2,061	20,176

5)

614,729	630,281	605,202	672,051

6)

35,903	38,319	43,732	4,276

7)

122,034	129,683	126,741	125,723

8)

14,658	10,450	14,065	14,560

Arrange the numbers from greatest to least.

1)

235,972	235,026	235,961	235,182

2)

7,481	7,812	7,418	7,408

3)

985	908	958	955

4)

61,751	60,302	69,712	62,392

5)

4,073	40,581	47,298	4,918

6)

76,403	70,621	74,062	73,640

7)

654,032	600,562	623,056	650,324

8)

183	1,180	1,308	1,003

Score | /

Date: _____

Arrange the numbers from greatest to least.

1)

90,783	9,304	19,761	91,451

2)

169,712	160,975	166,048	164,408

3)

732,009	739,236	738,028	733,004

4)

4,903	40,009	4,093	4,300

5)

59,032	51,043	56,216	57,628

6)

81,078	89,381	84,512	86,003

7)

374,192	371,645	307,526	370,682

8)

893	8,093	8,903	8,930

Ordering Digits

When given a certain number of digits, we can arrange the digits to form a certain number.

With these given four digits, we can form 2-digit numbers like 10, 61, 76 and 71; or 3-digit numbers like 106, 167, 670 and 761, or 4-digit like 1,067, 7,601, 6,710 and 6,701.

06 is not a 2-digit number, nor is 076 a 3-digit number.

Greatest 4-digit number is 7,610.
Smallest 4-digit number is 1,067 (Note: 0167 is a 3-digit number)

Use the given digits to form a) the greatest 4-digit and b) the smallest 4-digit number.

1)

a) ____6,530____   b) ____3,056____

2)

    8   2   6   3

a) _____   b) _____

3)

    0   9   1   4

a) _____   b) _____

Score   /

Date: _____

Use the given digits to form a) the greatest 4-digit and b) the smallest 4-digit number.

1)

    a) _____   b) _____

2)

    a) _____   b) _____

3)

    a) _____   b) _____

4)

    a) _____   b) _____

5)

    a) _____   b) _____

Use the given digits to form a) the greatest 5-digit and b) the smallest 5-digit number.

1)

a) _____   b) _____

2)

a) _____   b) _____

3)

a) _____   b) _____

4)

a) _____   b) _____

5)

a) _____   b) _____

Use the given digits to form a) the greatest 6-digit and b) the smallest 6-digit number.

1)

a) _____   b) _____

2)

a) _____   b) _____

3)

a) _____   b) _____

4)

a) _____   b) _____

5)

a) _____   b) _____

Number Patterns

Complete the number patterns.

1) 320 420 520 620 *720* 820

(+100)

2) 13,426 13,436 13,446 13,456 13,466 13,476

(+10)

3) 2,372 3,372 4,372 5,372 6,372 7,372

(+1,000)

4) [ ] 5,145 [ ] [ ] 5,148 5,149

5) [ ] 41,373 41,473 [ ] 41,673 [ ]

6) 11,421 [ ] [ ] 41,421 51,421 [ ]

7) [ ] 74,920 74,930 [ ] 74,950 [ ]

8) [ ] [ ] 9,273 9,274 [ ] 9,276

9) 23,156 24,156 [ ] 26,156 [ ] [ ]

10) [ ] 12,309 12,409 [ ] 12,609 [ ]

Date: _____

Complete the number patterns.

1) | 1,240 | 1,250 | | 1,270 | | 1,290 |

2) | 6,120 | | 6,320 | 6,420 | | 6,620 |

3) | 40,824 | 40,834 | | 40,854 | | |

4) | | 9,354 | 9,355 | | 9,357 | |

5) | 11,283 | | 13,283 | 14,283 | | 16,283 |

6) | 427 | | 627 | 727 | | 927 |

7) | | 83,045 | 84,045 | | 86,045 | |

8) | 37,128 | | 37,148 | | 37,168 | 37,178 |

9) | 10,921 | 20,921 | | | | 60,921 |

10) | | 4,196 | | 6,196 | | 8,196 |

Complete the number patterns.

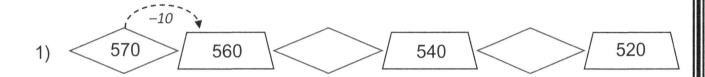

1) 570 560 [ ] 540 [ ] 520

2) 21,989 [ ] 21,789 21,689 [ ] 21,489

3) [ ] 4,978 [ ] 4,976 4,975 [ ]

4) [ ] 62,500 52,500 [ ] 32,500 [ ]

5) 7,398 7,388 [ ] [ ] 7,358 7,348

6) [ ] 30,531 29,531 [ ] 27,531 [ ]

7) 867 [ ] 847 837 [ ] 817

8) [ ] 9,810 [ ] 9,610 9,510 [ ]

9) [ ] 50,878 [ ] [ ] 50,875 50,874

10) 2,482 [ ] [ ] 2,452 2,442 [ ]

Score /   Date: _____

Complete the number patterns.

1) [ ]   6,731   [ ]   6,751   [ ]   6,771

2) 993   ♥   973   963   ♥   943

3) [ ]   27,485   [ ]   25,485   24,485   [ ]

4) ♥   32,876   32,875   ♥   32,873   ♥

5) 19,403   20,403   [ ]   [ ]   23,403   24,403

6) ♥   8,230   8,240   ♥   8,260   ♥

7) 289   [ ]   489   589   [ ]   789

8) ♥   3,158   ♥   3,156   3,155   ♥

9) [ ]   56,201   [ ]   [ ]   53,201   52,201

10) 7,200   ♥   ♥   7,500   7,600   ♥

Renaming & Regrouping Place Values

We can use place value patterns to rename a number.

As one factor increases by a place value, the other factor decreases by a place value, so the product remains the same. In whole numbers, we have previously learned renaming and regrouping of whole numbers as follows:

Thousands	Hundreds	Tens	Ones	Expanded Form
2	0	0	0	2 x 1,000 = 2 thousands
2	0	0	0	20 x 100 = 20 hundreds
2	0	0	0	200 x 10 = 200 tens
2	0	0	0	2,000 x 1 = 2,000 ones

Examples of regrouping and renaming:

Example 1

6,300
= 6 thousands + 3 hundreds
= 60 hundreds + 3 hundreds
= 63 hundreds

Example 2

475
= 4 hundreds + 7 tens + 5 ones
= 40 tens + 7 tens + 5 ones
= 47 tens[1] + 5 ones
= 46 tens + 15 ones

= 4 hundreds + 6 tens[2] + 15 ones
= 4 hundreds + 5 tens + 25 ones

= 3 hundreds[3] + 17 tens + 5 ones
= 2 hundreds + 27 tens + 5 ones

[1] 47 tens = 46 tens + 1 ten = 46 tens + 10 ones
[2] 6 tens = 5 tens + 1 ten = 5 tens + 10 ones
[3] 3 hundreds = 2 hundreds + 1 hundred = 2 hundreds + 10 tens

Example 3

8,609
= 8 thousands + 6 hundreds + 9 ones
= 8 thousands + 5 hundreds + 10 tens + 9 ones
= 8 thousands + 5 hundreds + 9 tens + 19 ones
= 8 thousands + 4 hundreds + 19 tens + 19 ones

= 8 thousands + 60 tens + 9 ones
= 7 thousands + 10 hundreds + 60 tens + 9 ones
= 7 thousands + 9 hundreds + 70 tens + 9 ones

= 86 hundreds + 9 ones
= 85 hundreds + 10 tens + 9 ones
= 85 hundreds + 9 tens + 19 ones

Example 4

3 thousands 17 hundreds 27 tens 8 ones
= 3 thousands + 1 thousand 7 hundreds + 2 hundreds 7 tens + 8 ones
= 4 thousands + 9 hundreds + 7 tens + 8 ones
= 4,978

Rename the numbers. Fill in the blanks with thousands, hundreds, tens or ones.

1) 58,400

   = 5 _____ + 8 _____ + 4 hundreds

   = 50 thousands + 8 _____ + 4 hundreds

   = 58 _____ + 4 hundreds

   = 580 _____ + 4 hundreds

   = 584 _____

   = 5,840 _____

2) 623,700

   = 623 _____ + 7 hundreds

   = 622 _____ + 10 hundreds + 7 hundreds

   = 622 hundreds + 17 _____

Rename the numbers. Fill in the blanks with thousands, hundreds, tens or ones.

1) 19,280

= 19 _____ + 2 hundreds + 8 _____

= 19 _____ + 20 _____ + 8 _____

= 19 _____ + 28 _____

= 190 _____ + 28 _____

= 1,900 _____ + 28 _____

= 1,928 _____

2) 493,600

= 493 _____ + 6 hundreds

= 4,930 _____ + 6 hundreds

= 4,936 _____

3) 820,500

= 8 _____ + 20 _____ + 5 hundreds

= 820 _____ + 5 hundreds

= 8,205 _____

4) 27,410

= 27 _____ + 4 hundreds + 1 _____

= 274 _____ + 1 _____

= 2,740 _____ + 1 _____

= 2,741 _____

Score   /

Date: _____

Rename the numbers. Fill in the blanks with thousands, hundreds, tens or ones.

1) 532,190

= 532 _____ + 1 hundred + 9 _____

= 5,320 _____ + 10 _____ + 9 _____

= 5,320 _____ + 19 _____

= 5,319 _____ + 29 _____

= 5,318 _____ + 30 _____

2) 493,600

= 493 _____ + 6 hundreds

= 4,930 _____ + 6 hundreds

= 4,936 _____

3) 382,100

= 382 _____ + 1 hundred

= 380 thousands + 2 _____ + 1 hundred

= 380 thousands + 20 _____ + 1 hundred

= 380 thousands + 21 _____

4) 27,430

= 27 _____ + 4 hundreds + 3 _____

= 274 _____ + 3 _____

= 2,740 _____ + 3 _____

= 2,743 _____

Rename the numbers. Fill in the blanks with thousands, hundreds, tens or ones.

1) 5,783

= 5 _____ + 7 _____ + 8 _____ + 3 ones

= 50 _____ + 7 _____ + 83 _____

= 57 _____ + 83 _____

= 570 _____ + 83 _____

= 569 _____ + 93 _____

= 568 _____ + 103 _____

2) 36,894

= 36 thousands + 8 _____ + 9 _____ + 4 _____

= 35 thousands + 18 _____ + 9 _____ + 4 _____

= 35 thousands + 17 _____ + 19 _____ + 4 _____

= 35 thousands + 17 _____ + 190 _____ + 4 _____

= 35 thousands + 17 _____ + 194 _____

3) 561,408

= 561 _____ + 4 _____ + 8 _____

= 560 _____ + 14 _____ + 8 _____

= 560 _____ + 13 _____ + 10 _____ + 8 _____

= 560 _____ + 13 _____ + 108 _____

4) 6,825

= 68 _____ + 2 _____ + 5 _____

= 67 _____ + 12 _____ + 5 _____

= 67 _____ + 120 _____ + 5 _____

= 67 _____ + 125 _____

Score _____ / _____

Date: _____

Fill in the blanks.

1)   780 = _____ tens

2)   50,000 + 4,000 + 90 + 3 = _____

3)   620 tens = _____ ones

4)   3 thousands + 9 hundreds + 7 tens = _____ tens

5)   2 hundreds 14 tens = _____

6)   4,589 tens = _____ hundreds _____ tens

7)   82,763 = _____ + 2,000 + 700 + 60 + 3

8)   3,600 tens = _____ thousands

9)   25 hundreds 6 tens 8 ones = _____

10)   700,000 + 90,000 + 5,000 + 600 + 8 = _____

11)   93 thousands 81 tens 27 ones = _____

12)   78,892 = 70,000 + _____ + 800 + 90 + 2

Fill in the blanks.

1) 9 thousands 15 hundreds 38 ones = _____

2) 46,000 = 3 thousands _____ hundreds

3) 79,000 + 8,000 + 600 + 50 + 2 = _____

4) 6,890 hundreds = _____ thousands

5) 5 ten thousands 3 thousands 24 hundreds 7 ones = _____

6) 9,457 tens = _____ hundreds 7 tens

7) 790 is _____ tens more 850

8) 93,000 + 700 + 86 = _____

9) 6,540 tens = _____ hundreds

10) 29 thousands 31 hundreds 8 tens 2 ones = _____

11) 35,893 = 35,000 + _____ + 93

12) 62,800 = 60 thousands _____ tens

Score [/]

Fill in the blanks.

1) $630,000 + 12,000 + 700 + 34 =$ _____

2)   870 hundreds = _____ thousands

3)   870 hundreds = _____ tens

4) $93,500 =$ 92 thousands _____ hundreds

5)   3,450 tens = _____ hundreds

6)   7 thousands 12 hundreds 8 tens 25 ones = _____

7) $36,000 + 1,590 =$ _____ tens

8)   14 thousands 23 hundreds 19 tens = _____ tens

9)   5,892 hundreds = _____ thousands 2 hundreds

10) $16,000 + 2,400 +$ _____ $+ 23 = 18,963$

11)   2,783 tens = 20 thousands _____ hundreds 3 tens

12)   34 hundreds 27 ones = _____

Rounding Numbers

Rounding numbers make them 'easier' to use or understand while also keeping them close to their original values. It gives us an estimate.

After rounding to nearest thousands, the rounded numbers will have digits to the right of the thousands place value with only zeros, irrespective if the numbers have been rounded up or down e.g. 7,000 for the number 6,782.

Method 1: Using the digit to the right of the place value

Step 1: Underline the digit to round

Step 2: Look at the digit to its right; if that digit is between 1 and 4, round down, and if between 5 and 9, round up.

Step 3: Replace the digit, and all the digits to the right with zeros

0	1	2	3	4	5	6	7	8	9
Round down					Round up				

Method 2: Using number line

With number line, we can visually see whether a value should be rounded up or down.

Step 1: Placing the place value being rounded by on either far end of the number line

Step 2: Locate the points representing the digits, and the midpoint on the number line. For points closer to the left and lesser than the midpoint, the number rounds down. And for points from midpoint to the right, the number rounds up.

Example 1: Rounding to the **nearest tens**.

Rounding 5$\underline{2}$3	Rounding 5$\underline{2}$8
Since ones place is 3, we round down tens place value to 2. The nearest tens is 520.	Since ones place is 8, we round up tens place value to 3. The nearest tens is 530.

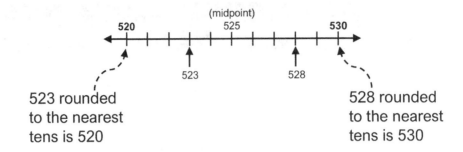

523 rounded
to the nearest
tens is 520

528 rounded
to the nearest
tens is 530

Example 2: Rounding to the **nearest hundreds**.

Rounding 2,7̲38	Rounding 2,7̲53
Since tens place is 3, we round down hundreds place value to 7. The nearest hundreds is 2,700.	Since tens place is 5, we round up hundreds place value to 8. The nearest hundreds is 2,800.

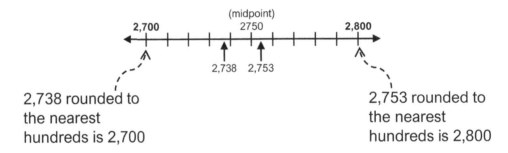

2,738 rounded to
the nearest
hundreds is 2,700

2,753 rounded to
the nearest
hundreds is 2,800

Example 3: Rounding to the **nearest thousands**.

Rounding 4̲2,378	Rounding 4̲2,813
Since hundreds place is 3, we round down thousands place value to 2. The nearest hundreds is 42,000.	Since hundreds place is 8, we round up thousands place value to 3. The nearest thousands is 43,000.

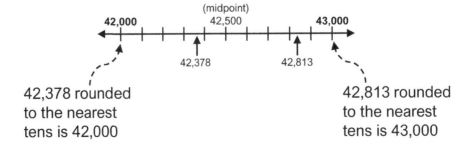

42,378 rounded
to the nearest
tens is 42,000

42,813 rounded
to the nearest
tens is 43,000

Round to the nearest tens.

1) 571   → | 570 | 5) 34,852   → | |

2) 93   → | | 6) 217,848 → | |

3) 4,156   → | | 7) 65   → | |

4) 128   → | | 8) 539,673 → | |

Round to the nearest hundreds.

9) 4,764   → | 4,800 | 13) 802   → | |

10) 129,451 → | | 14) 12,693   → | |

11) 736   → | | 15) 385,826 → | |

12) 41,032 → | | 16) 918   → | |

Round to the nearest thousands.

17) 35,873 → | 36,000 | 21) 5,261   → | |

18) 132,047 → | | 22) 439,984 → | |

19) 281,621 → | | 23) 692,507 → | |

20) 700,286 → | | 24) 8,438   → | |

Score   /

Date: _____

Round to the nearest hundreds.

1)   8,147   →   ☐   5)   23,056   →   ☐

2)   75,693   →   ☐   6)   1,026   →   ☐

3)   30,820   →   ☐   7)   492   →   ☐

4)   98,301   →   ☐   8)   70,621   →   ☐

Round to the nearest thousands.

9)   315,034   →   ☐   13)   73,249   →   ☐

10)   60,912   →   ☐   14)   832,745   →   ☐

11)   57,852   →   ☐   15)   2,395   →   ☐

12)   194,270   →   ☐   16)   243,518   →   ☐

Round to the nearest ten thousands.

17)   92,041   →   ☐   21)   814,578   →   ☐

18)   488,269   →   ☐   22)   27,527   →   ☐

19)   235,042   →   ☐   23)   12,693   →   ☐

20)   60,535   →   ☐   24)   859,073   →   ☐

Round to the nearest thousands.

1) 3,892 → [ ]

2) 12,276 → [ ]

3) 659,478 → [ ]

4) 90,721 → [ ]

5) 816,351 → [ ]

6) 5,174 → [ ]

7) 702,801 → [ ]

8) 21,753 → [ ]

Round to the nearest ten thousands.

9) 276,014 → [ ]

10) 58,371 → [ ]

11) 30,326 → [ ]

12) 844,167 → [ ]

13) 195,300 → [ ]

14) 32,636 → [ ]

15) 83,512 → [ ]

16) 91,183 → [ ]

Round to the nearest hundred thousands.

17) 792,680 → [ ]

18) 253,627 → [ ]

19) 812,439 → [ ]

20) 146,592 → [ ]

21) 930,751 → [ ]

22) 671,582 → [ ]

23) 503,845 → [ ]

24) 426,481 → [ ]

Score ___/___

Date: _____

Additions and Subtractions

The reasonableness of an answer can be assessed using mental computation and estimation strategies, like **rounding**.

Example 1: 46,985 + 2,739

Since the two addends are in ten thousands and thousands, we can round both to <u>nearest thousands</u>.

Round 46,985 → 47,000

Round 2,739 → 3,000

$$\begin{array}{r} {}^{1}47,000 \\ +\quad 3,000 \\ \hline 50,000 \end{array}$$ Estimate

Example 2: 46,985 + 829

As the second addend is in hundreds, we can round it to <u>nearest hundreds</u>.

Round 46,985 → 47,000

Round 829 → 800

$$\begin{array}{r} 47,000 \\ +\quad 800 \\ \hline 47,800 \end{array}$$ Estimate

Additions with Regrouping

An addition problem consists of the addends and the sum. It can be represented visually using number bonds.

6,985 + 1,246 = ?

addend addend sum

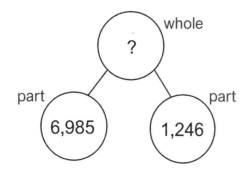

Using number bond, 6,985 and 1,246 are the parts and when added, we get the whole.

When adding, we stack the numbers and align them by place values. We add them column by column from the ones place from right to left. For each place value, when the sum is ten or more, we regroup to the place value to its left.

6,985 + 1,246

$$\begin{array}{r} 7,000 \\ +\quad 1,000 \\ \hline 8,000 \end{array}$$ Estimate

$$\begin{array}{r} 6,985 \\ +\quad 1,246 \\ \hline \end{array}$$

6,985 (part or addend)

1,246 (part or addend)

(whole or sum)

Ones	5+6=11	11 ones: Regroup 11 ones to 1 ten 1 one	
Tens	1+8+4=13	13 tens: Regroup13 tens to 1 hundred 3 tens	
Hundreds	1+9+2=12	12 hundreds: Regroup 12 hundreds to 1 thousand 2 hundreds	
Thousands	1+6+1=8	8 thousands	

Thousands Hundreds Tens Ones

$$\begin{array}{r} \overset{1}{}\overset{1}{9}\overset{1}{8}5 \\ 6,985 \\ +1,246 \\ \hline 8,231 \end{array}$$

8,231 is reasonable based on our estimate of 8,000.

Estimate the numbers. Add and check the reasonableness of the answer with the estimate.

1)
$$\begin{array}{r} 128{,}000 \\ +460{,}000 \\ \hline 588{,}000 \end{array}$$
$$\begin{array}{r} \overset{1}{1}\overset{1}{2}\overset{1}{8}\overset{1}{4}52 \\ +459748 \\ \hline 588{,}200 \end{array}$$

2)
$$\begin{array}{r} 287551 \\ +398592 \\ \hline \end{array}$$

3)
$$\begin{array}{r} 217136 \\ +330756 \\ \hline \end{array}$$

4)
$$\begin{array}{r} 271484 \\ +211581 \\ \hline \end{array}$$

5)
$$\begin{array}{r} 261991 \\ +24622 \\ \hline \end{array}$$

6)
$$\begin{array}{r} 275577 \\ +232603 \\ \hline \end{array}$$

7)
$$\begin{array}{r} 300{,}477 \\ +122{,}012 \\ \hline \end{array}$$

8)
$$\begin{array}{r} 380{,}098 \\ +447{,}814 \\ \hline \end{array}$$

Score   /   Date: _____

Estimate the numbers. Add and check the reasonableness of the answer with the estimate.

1)
$$257126 + 275483$$

2)
$$277443 + 144070$$

3)
$$321999 + 445495$$

4)
$$298278 + 331388$$

5)
$$359300 + 192307$$

6)
$$347965 + 332084$$

7)
$$324294 + 37700$$

8)
$$203148 + 97947$$

9)
$$259116 + 37523$$

10)
$$292119 + 77312$$

11)
$$263,498 + 44,986$$

12)
$$401,059 + 6,835$$

Estimate the numbers. Add and check the reasonableness of the answer with the estimate.

1)
```
    1 4 8 1 2 1
+   3 8 1 5 6 6
```

2)
```
    1 9 7 9 4 4
+     8 1 6 7 8
```

3)
```
    1 6 9,5 2 7
+   4 3 4,3 9 2
```

4)
```
    3 3 2,9 3 4
+     7 6 5 5 2
```

5)
```
    3 9 2 9 1 8
+     9 1 6 4 7
```

6)
```
    3 7 8 1 1 6
+   1 4 4 5 2 2
```

7)
```
    3 3 2 3 2 0
+   3 0 8 5 1 0
```

8)
```
    2 8 2 1 7 8
+   2 2 0 8 0 3
```

9)
```
    2 8 6 0 1 8
+   4 0 7 9 2 8
```

10)
```
    3 5 5 1 1 4
+   3 5 6 2 2 7
```

11)
```
    2 9 3 2 2 3
+   1 3 4 4 6 2
```

12)
```
    4 1 3 4 1 2
+   2 8 6 6 5 9
```

Score | /

Date: _____

Estimate the numbers. Add and check the reasonableness of the answer with the estimate.

1)
$$\begin{array}{r} 1\ 8\ 3\ 2\ 9\ 5 \\ +\ \ \ \ 6\ 3\ 0\ 5\ 8 \\ \hline \end{array}$$

2)
$$\begin{array}{r} 1\ 7\ 5\ 4\ 2\ 9 \\ +\ 2\ 3\ 2\ 9\ 2\ 7 \\ \hline \end{array}$$

3)
$$\begin{array}{r} 3\ 4\ 0\ 4\ 3\ 5 \\ +\ \ \ 9\ 3\ 1\ 7\ 2 \\ \hline \end{array}$$

4)
$$\begin{array}{r} 3\ 1\ 7\ 4\ 1\ 3 \\ +\ 1\ 5\ 9\ 9\ 0\ 3 \\ \hline \end{array}$$

5)
$$\begin{array}{r} 3\ 0\ 3\ 8\ 1\ 0 \\ +\ 2\ 1\ 4\ 3\ 8\ 1 \\ \hline \end{array}$$

6)
$$\begin{array}{r} 1\ 3\ 5\ 0\ 6\ 6 \\ +\ 4\ 7\ 9\ 4\ 4\ 7 \\ \hline \end{array}$$

7)
$$\begin{array}{r} 1\ 5\ 7\ 2\ 0\ 5 \\ +\ \ \ 5\ 3\ 7\ 1\ 5 \\ \hline \end{array}$$

8)
$$\begin{array}{r} 3\ 0\ 5\ 2\ 3\ 3 \\ +\ 1\ 6\ 8\ 0\ 1\ 8 \\ \hline \end{array}$$

9)
$$\begin{array}{r} 2\ 1\ 3\ 5\ 3\ 3 \\ +\ 3\ 5\ 2\ 1\ 3\ 7 \\ \hline \end{array}$$

10)
$$\begin{array}{r} 3\ 9\ 9\ 8\ 6\ 7 \\ +\ 1\ 6\ 9\ 0\ 2\ 2 \\ \hline \end{array}$$

11)
$$\begin{array}{r} 3\ 0\ 3,6\ 0\ 8 \\ +\ 1\ 6\ 3,2\ 8\ 9 \\ \hline \end{array}$$

12)
$$\begin{array}{r} 3\ 4\ 4,3\ 2\ 3 \\ +\ 4\ 6\ 7,6\ 1\ 5 \\ \hline \end{array}$$

Estimate the numbers. Add and check the reasonableness of the answer with the estimate.

1)
```
    2 7 1 6 2
    3 5 3 0 8
+ 2 5 9 2 4 4
```

2)
```
      8 5 2 9 2
    1 8 9 8 5 2
+ 2 4 0 4 7 0
```

3)
```
    2 6 2 1 2 5
      8 0 9 6 9
+ 2 5 2 0 2 3
```

4)
```
    1 0 0 0 7 1
      8 9 2 4 8
+ 1 0 9 8 1 5
```

5)
```
    1 6 9 2 9 6
    1 1 0 6 7 0
+ 2 0 7 3 5 6
```

6)
```
    2 4 8 1 6 0
    2 5 4 7 5 4
+ 1 5 0 0 1 1
```

7)
```
    2 4 6 1 9 7
      4 1 0 0 5
+ 1 6 4 4 3 8
```

8)
```
    2 5 7 9 3 2
    1 8 3 6 0 8
+   8 7 4 8 3
```

9)
```
    2 2 9 0 3 0
    1 3 0 8 5 1
+ 1 9 6 8 3 7
```

10)
```
      3 1 2 5 6
    1 6 2 9 5 2
+ 1 9 6 5 1 8
```

11)
```
    2 3 0 6 2 9
    2 9 5 5 1 9
+ 2 7 7 3 2 3
```

12)
```
    2 8 4 9 8 8
      2 4 6 1 6
+   5 5 1 2 4
```

Score   /

Date: _____

Estimate the numbers. Add and check the reasonableness of the answer with the estimate.

1)
```
    2 1 5 4 8 3
    1 4 7 9 6 4
+   1 4 4 9 4 1
```

2)
```
    2 5 9 4 1 9
    1 0 8 0 4 1
+   2 1 5 5 8 7
```

3)
```
    1 1 5 4 3 3
      6 7 6 4 2
+   1 9 8 9 5 0
```

4)
```
    1 1 1 0 3 6
    1 2 8 6 9 5
+   1 0 0 3 6 8
```

5)
```
      6 3 9 0 6
      1 9 1 8 5
+   2 8 7 8 0 6
```

6)
```
    2 2 4 3 0 4
      9 3 2 9 2
+   1 5 8 0 1 5
```

7)
```
    1 3 0 1 5 9
    1 6 7 8 6 4
+   1 0 3 9 0 2
```

8)
```
    2 8 4 6 0 8
      5 3 0 2 5
+   2 2 4 3 3 2
```

9)
```
    2 0 6 6 3 9
    2 7 3 3 6 3
+       3 5 9 7
```

10)
```
      5 3 9 7 3
      6 9 0 9 4
+   2 1 0 0 3 5
```

11)
```
      6 2 1 5 4
    2 6 7 4 2 2
+   1 3 5 7 0 6
```

12)
```
      1 0 6 9 0
    2 8 0 0 2 7
+     7 4 4 5 3
```

Estimate the numbers. Add and check the reasonableness of the answer with the estimate.

1)
```
    2 6 2 4 5 3
    1 0 4 8 8 9
+   1 6 4 9 1 4
```

2)
```
    1 3 4 7 5 8
    1 1 1 3 1 7
+       7 8 9 7
```

3)
```
    1 4 1 9 2 9
    2 2 4 4 6 4
+   2 1 2 0 1 3
```

4)
```
    2 1 7 6 1 5
    1 0 3 8 5 8
+     4 5 2 7 3
```

5)
```
      8 7 0 3 9
    2 3 0 7 4 6
+   1 4 6 1 0 3
```

6)
```
    1 6 0 0 4 8
    1 6 1 5 2 6
+   1 9 2 3 3 2
```

7)
```
    1 0 0 9 2 9
    1 3 4 6 3 3
+     3 1 4 2 3
```

8)
```
      4 8 2 5 4
    1 1 7 7 6 5
+     7 4 7 8 1
```

9)
```
    2 2 3 4 3 8
    2 3 6 5 9 6
+   2 0 6 2 8 6
```

10)
```
    2 9 4 6 5 2
    2 0 7 0 6 3
+     5 8 2 5 2
```

11)
```
    1 6 6 8 0 7
    1 5 0 2 1 0
+   1 6 0 1 0 6
```

12)
```
    2 5 4 2 6 8
      9 0 1 9 8
+   2 6 8 2 5 3
```

Score | /

Date: _____

Checking Validity of the Sum

$1\overset{1}{2},823$
$+\ 76,951$
———————
$89,774$

To check if the sum of 89,774 in this addition problem is correct, we use subtraction.

Subtract one addend from the sum:
89,774 – 76,951

$8\overset{8}{\cancel{9}},\overset{1}{7}74$
$-\ 76,951$
———————
$12,823$

Or 89,774 – 12,823

$8\overset{8}{\cancel{9}},\overset{1}{7}74$
$-\ 12,823$
———————
$76,951$

Subtracting one addend from the sum we get the value of the other addend. Thus, the sum of 89,774 is mostly like to be valid.

Estimate the numbers. Add and check the reasonableness of the answer with the estimate. Use the grid to check validity of the answer.

1)　
$$132807$$
$$+\quad 34365$$

2)　
$$284865$$
$$+\ 440951$$

3)
$$217539$$
$$+\ 285194$$

Estimate the numbers. Add and check the reasonableness of the answer with the estimate. Use the grid to check the validity of the answer.

1)

$$\begin{array}{r} 2\ 3\ 1\ 5\ 4\ 7 \\ +\ 1\ 8\ 7\ 5\ 1\ 3 \\ \hline \end{array}$$

2)

$$\begin{array}{r} 3\ 4\ 4\ 4\ 5\ 8 \\ +\ \ \ 1\ 7\ 4\ 6\ 3 \\ \hline \end{array}$$

3)

$$\begin{array}{r} 4\ 0\ 2\ 3\ 2\ 3 \\ +\ 2\ 2\ 6\ 8\ 6\ 6 \\ \hline \end{array}$$

4)

$$\begin{array}{r} 3\ 2\ 5\ 9\ 8\ 4 \\ +\ 2\ 7\ 5\ 8\ 2\ 3 \\ \hline \end{array}$$

5)

$$\begin{array}{r} 2\ 7\ 8\ 3\ 7\ 2 \\ +\ 3\ 5\ 9\ 8\ 1\ 3 \\ \hline \end{array}$$

6)

$$\begin{array}{r} 1\ 8\ 3\ 1\ 1\ 4 \\ +\ 4\ 1\ 0\ 9\ 2\ 9 \\ \hline \end{array}$$

Score   /

Date: _____

Estimate the numbers. Add and check the reasonableness of the answer with the estimate. Use the grid to check the validity of the answer.

1)

$$\begin{array}{r} 3\ 2\ 0\ 2\ 6\ 8 \\ +\ 2\ 2\ 8\ 5\ 4\ 7 \\ \hline \end{array}$$

2)

$$\begin{array}{r} 1\ 4\ 7\ 8\ 5\ 7 \\ +\ 3\ 3\ 1\ 4\ 6\ 7 \\ \hline \end{array}$$

3)

$$\begin{array}{r} 4\ 0\ 5\ 8\ 1\ 2 \\ +\ \ \ \ 8\ 0\ 3\ 2\ 6 \\ \hline \end{array}$$

4)

$$\begin{array}{r} 2\ 3\ 8\ 1\ 0\ 2 \\ +\ 3\ 8\ 4\ 7\ 6\ 5 \\ \hline \end{array}$$

5)

$$\begin{array}{r} 2\ 3\ 5\ 9\ 0\ 3 \\ +\ 4\ 6\ 7\ 1\ 3\ 7 \\ \hline \end{array}$$

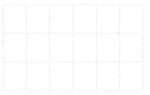

6)

$$\begin{array}{r} 3\ 0\ 0\ 7\ 3\ 7 \\ +\ 1\ 1\ 7\ 7\ 5\ 2 \\ \hline \end{array}$$

Estimate the numbers. Add and check the reasonableness of the answer with the estimate. Use the grid to check the validity of the answer.

1)
```
   2 7 7 4 4 3
+  1 4 4 0 7 0
```

2)
```
   2 9 8 2 7 8
+  3 3 1 3 8 8
```

3)
```
   3 4 7 9 6 5
+  3 3 2 0 8 4
```

4)
```
   2 0 3 1 4 8
+     9 7 9 4 7
```

5)
```
   2 9 2 1 1 9
+     7 7 3 1 2
```

6)
```
   4 0 1 0 5 9
+        6 8 3 5
```

Score | /

Date: _____

Subtractions with Regrouping

In a subtraction, the numbers are termed minuend, subtrahend and difference.

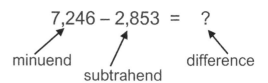

7,246 – 2,853 = ?

minuend   subtrahend   difference

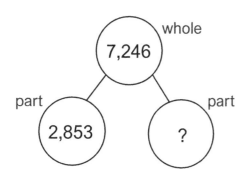

whole
7,246
part
2,853
part
?

In number bond, when the whole and one part is known, subtraction can be used to find the missing part. This missing part is the difference. When the whole is 7,246 and one part is 2,853, we subtract the known part from the whole i.e. 7,246 – 2,853.

We stack bigger numbers and align by place values to subtract them column by column.

We subtract from right to left, from the ones place. For each place value, when the digit in the minuend is less than the digit in the subtrahend, we regroup the digit to its left before subtracting.

Example 1: 7,246 – 2,853

```
  7,000
– 3,000
───────
  4,000
```

```
  7,246   (whole or minuend)
– 2,853   (part or subtrahend)
───────
          (part or difference)
```

Ones	Tens	Hundreds	Thou.
6 – 3 = 3	• 4 is smaller than 5 • Regroup 2 hund. 4 tens to 1 hund. 14 tens • 14 – 5 = 9	• 1 is smaller than 8 • Regroup 7 thous. 1 hund. to 6 thous. 11 hund. • 11 – 8 = 3	6 – 2 = 4

```
        Thousands Hundreds Tens Ones
     6     11  1
     7 , 2 4 6
   – 2 , 8 5 3
   ───────────
     4 , 3 9 3
```

4,393 is reasonable based on our estimate of 4,000.

When there is at least one zero in the minuend, we combine place values to regroup several digits together.

Example 2: 9,001 – 2,647

```
  9,000
– 3,000
───────
  6,000
```

```
  9,001   (whole or minuend)
– 2,647   (part or difference)
───────
          (part or subtrahend)
```

Score   /

Ones	Tens	Hunds.	Thous.
▪ 1 is smaller than 7 ▪ **Combine 3 place values and regroup 900 tens 1 one to 899 tens 11 ones** ▪ 11 − 7 = 4	9 − 4 = 5	9 − 6 = 3	8 − 2 = 6

Thousands Hundreds Tens Ones

8 9 9   1
9,001
− 2,647
6,354

6,354 is reasonable based on our estimate of 6,000.

Estimate the numbers. Then subtract them and check the reasonableness of the answer with the estimate.

1)
```
   2 14 1
  352,000
 − 67,000
  285,000
```
```
  2 14 1   7 1
 3 5 1 8 8 3
 −   6 7 2 7 7
 2 8 4,6 0 6
```

2)
```
 3 1 0 3 9 5
− 2 4 2 4 8 8
```

3)
```
 3 2 8 6 5 3
− 2 7 4 7 6 3
```

4)
```
 6 6 5 8 0 2
− 3 1 5 8 8 0
```

5)
```
 6 8 2 1 7 0
− 3 8 4 6 8 0
```

6)
```
 5 9 3 3 2 8
− 1 6 3 2 2 2
```

7)
```
 3 3 0 4 4 0
−   1 8 4 7 9
```

8)
```
 5 8 1 0 0 8
− 1 2 8 5 5 1
```

Score [/]   Date: _____

Estimate the numbers. Then subtract them and check the reasonableness of the answer with the estimate.

1)
$$\begin{array}{r} 408087 \\ -\ 270251 \\ \hline \end{array}$$

2)
$$\begin{array}{r} 664739 \\ -\ 349760 \\ \hline \end{array}$$

3)
$$\begin{array}{r} 385036 \\ -\ \ 84035 \\ \hline \end{array}$$

4)
$$\begin{array}{r} 421689 \\ -\ 211589 \\ \hline \end{array}$$

5)
$$\begin{array}{r} 309688 \\ -\ 120234 \\ \hline \end{array}$$

6)
$$\begin{array}{r} 314872 \\ -\ 247409 \\ \hline \end{array}$$

7)
$$\begin{array}{r} 495228 \\ -\ 283822 \\ \hline \end{array}$$

8)
$$\begin{array}{r} 428278 \\ -\ \ 78055 \\ \hline \end{array}$$

9)
$$\begin{array}{r} 567660 \\ -\ 198112 \\ \hline \end{array}$$

10)
$$\begin{array}{r} 625513 \\ -\ \ 43404 \\ \hline \end{array}$$

11)
$$\begin{array}{r} 515643 \\ -\ 364037 \\ \hline \end{array}$$

12)
$$\begin{array}{r} 584674 \\ -\ 302022 \\ \hline \end{array}$$

Estimate the numbers. Then subtract them and check the reasonableness of the answer with the estimate.

1)
```
  4 0 0 9 6 6
- 1 5 3 3 9 6
```

2)
```
  4 0 6 2 3 8
-     7 4 6 6
```

3)
```
  4 3 2 5 7 3
- 3 3 8 9 6 0
```

4)
```
  5 9 4 9 0 8
- 2 8 4 7 8 9
```

5)
```
  5 1 7 6 6 0
-   9 6 5 0 1
```

6)
```
  5 1 4 2 7 3
- 3 2 4 8 3 8
```

7)
```
  4 0 4 0 5 6
-     2 8 6 8
```

8)
```
  3 1 8 6 8 2
-   2 6 9 3 6
```

9)
```
  4 8 5 6 9 6
- 3 6 9 0 0 9
```

10)
```
  4 1 0 7 1 4
- 2 3 9 2 6 7
```

11)
```
  6 9 8 1 8 4
- 3 6 9 9 3 7
```

12)
```
  3 8 8 2 2 5
- 2 8 0 1 4 8
```

Score   /   Date: _____

Estimate the numbers. Then subtract them and check the reasonableness of the answer with the estimate.

1)
$$\begin{array}{r} 3\,1\,8\,8\,3\,3 \\ -\ 2\,7\,5\,6\,1\,9 \\ \hline \end{array}$$

2)
$$\begin{array}{r} 6\,0\,0\,2\,9\,1 \\ -\ \ \ 6\,2\,6\,8\,9 \\ \hline \end{array}$$

3)
$$\begin{array}{r} 6\,5\,1\,0\,8\,9 \\ -\ 1\,4\,7\,4\,6\,4 \\ \hline \end{array}$$

4)
$$\begin{array}{r} 4\,2\,0\,9\,3\,7 \\ -\ 2\,9\,7\,0\,0\,8 \\ \hline \end{array}$$

5)
$$\begin{array}{r} 3\,7\,8\,4\,6\,2 \\ -\ 2\,5\,5\,1\,7\,2 \\ \hline \end{array}$$

6)
$$\begin{array}{r} 3\,5\,8\,8\,3\,7 \\ -\ 2\,7\,8\,3\,9\,9 \\ \hline \end{array}$$

7)
$$\begin{array}{r} 4\,4\,0\,8\,9\,7 \\ -\ 3\,6\,0\,9\,0\,9 \\ \hline \end{array}$$

8)
$$\begin{array}{r} 3\,5\,2\,7\,5\,7 \\ -\ 2\,9\,0\,9\,3\,3 \\ \hline \end{array}$$

9)
$$\begin{array}{r} 5\,8\,8\,8\,0\,1 \\ -\ 2\,7\,0\,0\,7\,7 \\ \hline \end{array}$$

10)
$$\begin{array}{r} 5\,0\,5\,3\,0\,4 \\ -\ 1\,7\,5\,1\,4\,7 \\ \hline \end{array}$$

11)
$$\begin{array}{r} 4\,3\,0\,1\,2\,0 \\ -\ 3\,0\,2\,5\,3\,8 \\ \hline \end{array}$$

12)
$$\begin{array}{r} 4\,6\,9\,1\,1\,9 \\ -\ 2\,2\,2\,4\,5\,5 \\ \hline \end{array}$$

Checking Validity of the Difference

$$\begin{array}{r} {}^{4}{}_{1}5{}^{5}{}_{1} \\ \cancel{5}4,9\cancel{6}3 \\ - 36,839 \\ \hline 18,124 \end{array}$$

To check if the difference of 18,124 in this subtraction problem is valid, we use addition.

Add the difference to the subtrahend: 18,124 + 36,839

$$\begin{array}{r} {}^{1}{}^{1} \\ 1\,8,1\,2\,4 \\ + 3\,6,8\,3\,9 \\ \hline 5\,4,9\,6\,3 \end{array}$$

Estimate the numbers. Subtract and check the reasonableness of the answer with the estimate. Use the grid to check the validity of the answer.

1)

$$\begin{array}{r} 5\,2\,7\,0\,3\,8 \\ - 3\,6\,0\,2\,5\,0 \\ \hline \end{array}$$

2)

$$\begin{array}{r} 5\,1\,0\,0\,8\,8 \\ - 3\,2\,9\,1\,9\,8 \\ \hline \end{array}$$

3)

$$\begin{array}{r} 3\,1\,2\,8\,2\,5 \\ - 2\,7\,5\,5\,4\,1 \\ \hline \end{array}$$

4)

$$\begin{array}{r} 6\,1\,5\,5\,3\,3 \\ - 3\,4\,5\,9\,3\,6 \\ \hline \end{array}$$

Score   /   Date: _____

Estimate the numbers. Subtract and check the reasonableness of the answer with the estimate. Use the grid to check the validity of the answer.

1)

$$\begin{array}{r} 3\ 0\ 0\ 3\ 6\ 7 \\ -\ \ \ \ 1\ 4\ 1\ 0\ 9 \\ \hline \end{array}$$

2)

$$\begin{array}{r} 5\ 3\ 6\ 8\ 0\ 9 \\ -\ 3\ 9\ 9\ 3\ 5\ 3 \\ \hline \end{array}$$

3)

$$\begin{array}{r} 4\ 9\ 1\ 1\ 3\ 8 \\ -\ 3\ 3\ 9\ 1\ 7\ 0 \\ \hline \end{array}$$

4)

$$\begin{array}{r} 5\ 4\ 6\ 8\ 9\ 9 \\ -\ 1\ 3\ 2\ 1\ 4\ 1 \\ \hline \end{array}$$

5)

$$\begin{array}{r} 6\ 8\ 3\ 8\ 0\ 3 \\ -\ 3\ 9\ 7\ 4\ 7\ 7 \\ \hline \end{array}$$

6)

$$\begin{array}{r} 5\ 4\ 0\ 5\ 7\ 3 \\ -\ \ \ \ 7\ 8\ 8\ 3\ 5 \\ \hline \end{array}$$

Estimate the numbers. Subtract and check the reasonableness of the answer with the estimate. Use the grid to check the validity of the answer.

1)
$$
\begin{array}{r}
3\ 9\ 7\ 7\ 4\ 1 \\
-\ \ 3\ 0\ 4\ 8\ 1\ 9 \\
\hline
\end{array}
$$

2)
$$
\begin{array}{r}
6\ 4\ 4\ 8\ 9\ 9 \\
-\ \ 1\ 5\ 3\ 0\ 7\ 6 \\
\hline
\end{array}
$$

3)
$$
\begin{array}{r}
5\ 9\ 8\ 8\ 6\ 0 \\
-\ \ 1\ 5\ 4\ 6\ 1\ 9 \\
\hline
\end{array}
$$

4)
$$
\begin{array}{r}
6\ 2\ 9\ 2\ 8\ 6 \\
-\ \ \ \ 9\ 1\ 4\ 9\ 7 \\
\hline
\end{array}
$$

5)
$$
\begin{array}{r}
3\ 0\ 6\ 7\ 6\ 9 \\
-\ \ \ \ 4\ 3\ 7\ 8\ 8 \\
\hline
\end{array}
$$

6)
$$
\begin{array}{r}
4\ 2\ 0\ 2\ 8\ 0 \\
-\ \ 2\ 8\ 9\ 7\ 1\ 3 \\
\hline
\end{array}
$$

Score | /

Date: _____

Missing Numbers

Finding Addends

An addition problem consists of the addends and the sum.

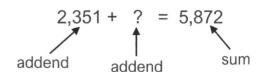

$$2{,}351 + \ ? \ = 5{,}872$$

addend   addend   sum

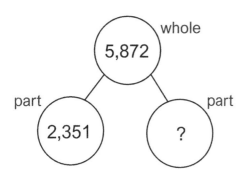

whole

5,872

part   2,351

part   ?

Using the terms of number bond, the addends are the parts, and the sum is the whole. Finding a missing addend is made easy when the concept of parts and whole is understood. The whole or sum is always the biggest of the three numbers.

To find the missing addend or part, we use subtraction. We subtract the known part from the whole. For example, 5,872 – 2,351 = 3,521.

Finding 2nd addend (part):

$$\begin{array}{r} 2\,1\,8\,,9\,5\,1 \\ + \qquad ? \\ \hline 2\,8\,3\,,3\,8\,7 \end{array}$$

(part or addend)
(part or addend)
(whole or sum)

$$\begin{array}{r} {\scriptstyle 7\ 1} \\ 28\!\!\!/3{,}000 \\ -\ 219{,}000 \\ \hline 64{,}000 \end{array}$$

	2	8	3	3	8	7
–	2	1	8	9	5	1
		6	4	4	3	6

$$\begin{array}{r} 2\,1\,8\,,9\,5\,1 \\ +\ \ 6\,4\,,4\,3\,6 \\ \hline 2\,8\,3\,,3\,8\,7 \end{array}$$

Finding 1st addend (part):

$$\begin{array}{r} ? \\ +\ 3\,1\,6\,,5\,2\,0 \\ \hline 5\,2\,6\,,4\,2\,8 \end{array}$$

(part or addend)
(part or addend)
(whole or sum)

$$\begin{array}{r} {\scriptstyle 1\ 1} \\ 52\!\!\!/6{,}000 \\ -\ 317{,}000 \\ \hline 209{,}000 \end{array}$$

	5	2	6	4	2	8
–	3	1	6	5	2	0
	2	0	9	9	0	8

$$\begin{array}{r} 2\,0\,9\,,9\,0\,8 \\ +\ 3\,1\,6\,,5\,2\,0 \\ \hline 5\,2\,6\,,4\,2\,8 \end{array}$$

Estimate the numbers. Then using the grid, find the missing addend and check the reasonableness of the answer with the estimate.

1)
```
    3 7 3,2 6 5
  + 2 9 3,8 6 4
    6 6 7 1 2 9
```

```
 5   1   6  10   1
 6   6   7   1   2   9
 3   7   3   2   6   5
 2   9   3   8   6   4
```

2)
```
    2 8 6,3 2 7
  + 1 6 5 8 5 8
    4 5 2 1 8 5
```

```
 3  14  11   1   7   1
 4   5   2   1   8   5
 1   6   5   8   5   8
 2   8   6   3   2   7
```

3)
```
    3 4 5 2 2 8
  + [        ]
    5 8 2 9 4 2
```

4)
```
  [        ]
  + 3 4 4 2 8 5
    7 5 5 2 8 8
```

5)
```
    1 7 1 6 4 9
  + [        ]
    3 2 3 3 3 0
```

6)
```
  [        ]
  + 2 3 7 5 9 2
    6 0 6 4 9 6
```

7)
```
    1 7 8 0 5 5
  + [        ]
    3 0 6 8 4 3
```

8)
```
  [        ]
  + 3 0 6 0 3 8
    7 1 8 8 7 2
```

9)
```
    1 6 6 3 4 5
  + [        ]
    3 4 5 8 8 3
```

10)
```
  [        ]
  + 2 7 3 7 5 2
    6 9 3 2 1 4
```

11)
```
    2 5 0 1 0 9
  + [        ]
    5 5 5 2 3 0
```

12)
```
  [        ]
  + 3 2 1 3 5 7
    4 7 5 8 5 3
```

Score /   Date: _____

Estimate the numbers. Then using the grid, find the missing addend and check the reasonableness of the answer with the estimate.

1)
```
    2 0 4 2 8 0
  + [          ]
    2 1 2 0 3 5
```

2)
```
    [          ]
  +     1 8 3 0 3
    2 7 7 0 0 0
```

3)
```
    3 0 8 7 5 1
  + [          ]
    4 6 8 5 4 7
```

4)
```
    [          ]
  + 2 0 4 8 1 7
    3 6 8 6 1 4
```

5)
```
    1 3 1 9 4 3
  + [          ]
    1 6 7 2 4 1
```

6)
```
    [          ]
  +     8 7 5 8 1
    3 8 3 5 7 3
```

7)
```
    2 8 5 2 3 8
  + [          ]
    5 4 0 0 2 4
```

8)
```
    [          ]
  + 4 7 2 8 4 0
    6 8 4 4 5 5
```

9)
```
    3 4 7 1 6 0
  + [          ]
    5 2 7 1 2 0
```

10)
```
    [          ]
  + 3 5 4 9 2 4
    5 2 3 5 7 7
```

11)
```
    2 8 4 9 3 6
  + [          ]
    5 0 1 6 8 6
```

12)
```
    [          ]
  +     2 5 5 4 0
    1 8 7 9 0 0
```

Estimate the numbers. Then using the grid, find the missing addend and check the reasonableness of the answer with the estimate.

1)
```
    3 5 8 3 0 2
  + [         ]
    7 4 2 1 7 2
```

2)
```
    [         ]
  +   7 0 8 2 8
    2 1 1 8 5 6
```

3)
```
    3 5 0 1 4 1
  + [         ]
    5 1 0 8 0 9
```

4)
```
    [         ]
  + 4 7 3 2 0 3
    7 8 5 4 0 7
```

5)
```
    3 8 7 7 6 9
  + [         ]
    8 6 8 6 1 1
```

6)
```
    [         ]
  + 3 2 9 8 6 7
    6 1 6 7 5 1
```

7)
```
    2 8 2 2 8 2
  + [         ]
    7 6 2 5 5 6
```

8)
```
    [         ]
  + 3 7 7 5 3 7
    6 1 7 2 3 0
```

9)
```
    1 8 7 5 7 0
  + [         ]
    6 3 4 7 3 3
```

10)
```
    [         ]
  +   2 7 6 0 2
    2 7 6 5 4 7
```

11)
```
    3 9 1 3 8 8
  + [         ]
    7 5 4 9 2 3
```

12)
```
    [         ]
  +   6 5 8 7 8
    2 3 4 1 5 3
```

Score ___/___   Date: _____

Estimate the numbers. Then using the grid, find the missing addend and check the reasonableness of the answer with the estimate.

1)
```
  1 3 8 0 7 2
+ [         ]
  ‾‾‾‾‾‾‾‾‾‾‾
  2 7 4 1 0 8
```

2)
```
  [         ]
+ 1 1 5 1 9 9
  ‾‾‾‾‾‾‾‾‾‾‾
  3 6 4 9 3 4
```

3)
```
  4 0 9 4 5 3
+ [         ]
  ‾‾‾‾‾‾‾‾‾‾‾
  5 4 9 1 3 3
```

4)
```
  [         ]
+ 2 1 3 7 8 6
  ‾‾‾‾‾‾‾‾‾‾‾
  5 8 4 2 0 2
```

5)
```
  3 6 5 5 6 5
+ [         ]
  ‾‾‾‾‾‾‾‾‾‾‾
  5 7 7 1 1 4
```

6)
```
  [         ]
+ 2 6 3 0 8 8
  ‾‾‾‾‾‾‾‾‾‾‾
  4 7 1 1 4 0
```

7)
```
  3 0 7 5 6 8
+ [         ]
  ‾‾‾‾‾‾‾‾‾‾‾
  5 2 4 5 8 0
```

8)
```
  [         ]
+ 3 5 5 9 1 0
  ‾‾‾‾‾‾‾‾‾‾‾
  5 7 5 7 0 8
```

9)
```
  3 4 9 9 9 5
+ [         ]
  ‾‾‾‾‾‾‾‾‾‾‾
  5 0 0 1 7 8
```

10)
```
  [         ]
+ 3 6 8 7 1 6
  ‾‾‾‾‾‾‾‾‾‾‾
  7 5 1 1 7 1
```

11)
```
  2 0 8 8 4 0
+ [         ]
  ‾‾‾‾‾‾‾‾‾‾‾
  6 8 9 6 0 0
```

12)
```
  [         ]
+ 2 0 1 6 8 7
  ‾‾‾‾‾‾‾‾‾‾‾
  4 5 4 2 6 1
```

Finding Minuend and Subtrahend

In a subtraction, the numbers are termed minuend, subtrahend and difference.

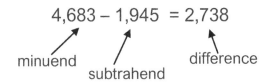

$$4,683 - 1,945 = 2,738$$

minuend   subtrahend   difference

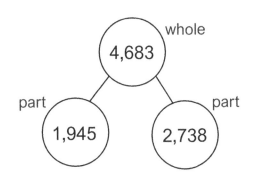

Minuend is the largest number of the three. Using the terms of the number bond, this is the whole. And the subtrahend and difference refer to the two parts.

Finding minuend (whole) is similar to an addition problem, we add the subtrahend to the difference.

Finding subtrahend or difference (part), we subtract the known part from the minuend.

Finding minuend (whole):

```
          ?        (whole)
   −  56,098       (part) ←
   ──────────              ⟍  We add the 2 parts
      31,149       (part) ←
```

56,000	5 6 0⁽¹⁾ 9⁽¹⁾ 8
− 31,000	+ 3 1 1 4 9
87,000	8 7 2 4 7

```
   87,247
 − 56,098
 ────────
   31,149
```

Finding subtrahend (part):

```
    82,374     (whole) ←
  −     ?      (part)     ⟍ We subtract known part
  ─────────               ⟋  from whole
    20,426     (part) ←
```

82,000	8 2̷⁽¹⁾ 3⁽¹⁾ 7̷⁽⁶⁾ 4⁽¹⁾
− 20,000	− 2 0 4 2 6
62,000	6 1 9 4 8

```
   82,374
 − 61,948
 ────────
   20,426
```

Score /

Date: _____

Estimate the numbers. Then using the grid, find the missing minuend or subtrahend and check the reasonableness of the answer with the estimate.

1)
```
   5 5 6 8 3 1
 -[2 3 0,5 2 4]
   3 2 6 3 0 7
```
5	5	6	8	²3̸	¹1
-3	2	6	3	0	7
2	3	0	5	2	4

2)
```
  [6 7 3,0 2 3]
 - 1 7 7 0 9 0
   4 9 5 9 3 3
```
¹4	¹9	¹5	¹9	3	3
+1	7	7	0	9	0
6	7	3	0	2	3

3)
```
   3 0 6 9 3 3
 -[           ]
   2 9 7 2 7 5
```

4)
```
  [           ]
 -     4 6 5 0 1
   6 4 4 4 3 4
```

5)
```
   4 5 0 7 7 3
 -[           ]
   4 2 4 3 7 3
```

6)
```
  [           ]
 - 1 5 9 4 0 2
   1 9 6 9 0 6
```

7)
```
   5 8 9 1 5 4
 -[           ]
   2 7 7 3 2 4
```

8)
```
  [           ]
 - 3 3 2 8 2 4
   1 8 6 4 8 1
```

9)
```
   5 0 6 2 5 5
 -[           ]
   4 1 5 3 3 0
```

10)
```
  [           ]
 - 3 7 8 7 6 2
   2 4 1 5 9 5
```

11)
```
   3 7 9 2 0 8
 -[           ]
   3 2 3 3 7 9
```

12)
```
  [           ]
 -     7 7 3 4 0
   4 7 3 8 5 2
```

Estimate the numbers. Then using the grid, find the missing minuend or subtrahend and check the reasonableness of the answer with the estimate.

1)
```
   6 8 2 2 1 0
 - [          ]
 ─────────────
   6 1 3 2 3 0
```

2)
```
   [          ]
 -   2 7 5 0 6 9
 ───────────────
     1 3 0 1 4 7
```

3)
```
   4 0 0 8 4 4
 - [          ]
 ─────────────
   3 4 8 2 0 1
```

4)
```
   [          ]
 -     5 4 4 2 0
 ───────────────
     3 4 5 8 9 5
```

5)
```
   5 9 9 6 8 6
 - [          ]
 ─────────────
   2 9 6 0 7 6
```

6)
```
   [          ]
 -   2 7 8 2 5 0
 ───────────────
       7 8 8 8 2
```

7)
```
   6 0 1 1 3 2
 - [          ]
 ─────────────
   4 1 0 5 8 3
```

8)
```
   [          ]
 -     9 5 9 6 1
 ───────────────
     5 8 3 5 4 6
```

9)
```
   3 4 4 1 1 2
 - [          ]
 ─────────────
     8 4 9 9 2
```

10)
```
   [          ]
 -     5 8 8 9 3
 ───────────────
     6 0 8 7 5 3
```

11)
```
   3 0 3 2 0 1
 - [          ]
 ─────────────
     8 7 5 2 7
```

12)
```
   [          ]
 -   1 7 6 1 4 4
 ───────────────
     3 0 4 6 2 2
```

Score | / |

Date: _____

Estimate the numbers. Then using the grid, find the missing minuend or subtrahend and check the reasonableness of the answer with the estimate.

1)
```
  4 2 8 0 2 1
–
  _____
    6 5 1 4 0
```

2)
```
  _____
–   1 8 8 2 8 9
  _____
    4 2 2 0 8 1
```

3)
```
  5 0 7 9 6 2
–
  _____
    2 4 1 3 0 0
```

4)
```
  _____
–   1 5 0 3 1 1
  _____
    3 3 3 7 1 0
```

5)
```
  4 6 1 2 3 7
–
  _____
    2 8 4 6 4 4
```

6)
```
  _____
–   1 6 0 4 9 2
  _____
    2 3 7 5 2 7
```

7)
```
  3 7 3 7 9 2
–
  _____
    3 3 6 5 2 2
```

8)
```
  _____
–   2 9 0 1 4 6
  _____
    1 0 9 1 1 6
```

9)
```
  4 2 0 7 7 4
–
  _____
    2 0 1 2 8 5
```

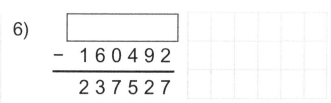

10)
```
  _____
–     4 0 2 1 4
  _____
    2 9 7 3 0 5
```

11)
```
  4 4 0 9 5 9
–
  _____
    6 3 0 1 8
```

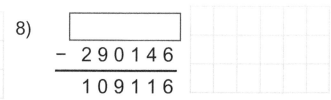

12)
```
  _____
–   2 9 7 7 9 0
  _____
    2 5 2 1 7 5
```

Finding Digits In Additions

Ones	8+4=12	12 ones = 1 ten 2 ones Regroup 1 to tens place
Tens	1+0+□=4	Missing digit is 3.
Hundreds	9+3=12	12 hundreds = 1 thousand 2 hundreds; Regroup 1 to thousands place.
Thousands	1+□+2=11	Sum shows 1, we can assume as 11 thousands. 11 thousands = 1 ten thousand 1 thousand. Regroup 1 to ten thousands. Missing digit is 8.
Ten Thousands	1+3+1=□	Missing digit is 5.

$$\begin{array}{r} {}^{1}\,{}^{1}3\;\boxed{8}\;9\;\overset{1}{0}\;8 \\ +\;1\;2\;3\;\boxed{3}\;4 \\ \hline \boxed{5}\;1\;2\;4\;2 \end{array}$$

Fill in the missing digits.

1)
$$\begin{array}{r} 4\;0\;3\;\square \\ +\;7\;\square\;9\;3 \\ \hline 1\;2\;0\;2\;7 \end{array}$$

2)
$$\begin{array}{r} 6\;0\;\square\;5 \\ +\;\square\;8\;0\;3 \\ \hline 1\;1\;8\;9\;8 \end{array}$$

3)
$$\begin{array}{r} 5\;2\;8\;8 \\ +\;2\;\square\;3\;\square \\ \hline 8\;0\;2\;3 \end{array}$$

4)
$$\begin{array}{r} 5\;\square\;9\;\square \\ +\;1\;4\;7\;1 \\ \hline 6\;8\;6\;5 \end{array}$$

5)
$$\begin{array}{r} 4\;3\;1\;7 \\ +\;\square\;1\;\square\;0 \\ \hline 1\;0\;4\;5\;7 \end{array}$$

6)
$$\begin{array}{r} 1\;\square\;0\;7 \\ +\;2\;7\;3\;\square \\ \hline 4\;4\;4\;1 \end{array}$$

7)
$$\begin{array}{r} 2\;0\;\square\;4 \\ +\;\square\;7\;1\;0 \\ \hline 6\;7\;6\;4 \end{array}$$

8)
$$\begin{array}{r} \square\;4\;7\;\square \\ +\;6\;3\;3\;3 \\ \hline 1\;0\;8\;1\;1 \end{array}$$

9)
$$\begin{array}{r} 1\;9\;\square\;9 \\ +\;1\;\square\;9\;2 \\ \hline 3\;9\;8\;1 \end{array}$$

10)
$$\begin{array}{r} \square\;0\;4\;\square \\ +\;7\;9\;2\;0 \\ \hline 9\;9\;6\;8 \end{array}$$

11)
$$\begin{array}{r} 2\;\square\;1\;4 \\ +\;6\;3\;5\;\square \\ \hline 8\;9\;6\;9 \end{array}$$

12)
$$\begin{array}{r} 3\;2\;4\;\square \\ +\;\square\;6\;6\;6 \\ \hline 1\;0\;9\;1\;3 \end{array}$$

Score   /   Date: _____

Fill in the missing digits.

```
1)      1 0 8 □ 9          2)      1 0 9 □ 6          3)        9 □ 8 9
    +       4 5 6 □            +     □ 6 0 8              +   2 0 7 9 □
    ───────────────         ──────────────────         ─────────────────
        1 5 □ 2 7               1 8 5 4 □                  3 □ 1 8 7
```

```
4)        9 8 □ 9          5)      □ 5 1 2          6)      1 □ 5 8 1
    +   1 □ 2 2 7              +   1 2 0 5 □            +   1 1 4 □ 2
    ───────────────         ─────────────────        ─────────────────
        2 5 □ 9 6               2 0 5 □ 1                2 2 □ 6 3
```

```
7)      1 □ 1 1 7          8)      1 0 □ 3 7          9)      1 1 9 7 □
    +   1 4 1 7 □              +   1 1 3 7 □              +     5 □ 6 4
    ───────────────         ──────────────────         ─────────────────
        2 5 2 □ 6               2 □ 3 1 2                  1 7 8 □ 2
```

```
10)       8 □ 0 2         11)      1 1 7 □ 3         12)      1 1 4 3 □
    +   2 2 1 □ 4              +   □ 2 4 5                +     6 □ 6 5
    ───────────────         ──────────────────         ─────────────────
        3 □ 0 4 6               1 6 0 2 □                  1 □ 2 0 0
```

```
13)     □ 0 1 5 4         14)      1 1 4 9 □         15)        9 6 □ 4
    +   1 4 5 □ 9              +   1 0 □ 8 1              +   □ 8 0 9
    ───────────────         ──────────────────         ─────────────────
        2 4 □ 3 3               2 1 6 □ 7                  1 5 4 3 □
```

```
16)     1 1 1 9 □         17)      □ 6 3 7          18)        8 □ 3 6
    +   1 □ 6 3 5              +   1 8 5 □ 3              +   1 5 0 □ 0
    ───────────────         ─────────────────        ─────────────────
        2 6 8 □ 9               2 8 2 3 □                  2 □ 5 2 6
```

Fill in the missing digits.

1)
```
    1 □ 9 2 9
  +   1 2 8 3 □
  ─────────────
    2 4 7 □ 5
```

2)
```
    □ 3 0 9
  +   2 0 0 □ 3
  ─────────────
    2 9 3 7 □
```

3)
```
    □ 5 0 5
  +   1 3 7 9 □
  ─────────────
    2 3 □ 9 7
```

4)
```
    9 4 9 □
  + 2 □ 3 9 6
  ─────────────
    2 9 8 □ 0
```

5)
```
    9 □ 5 6
  + 1 9 9 6 □
  ─────────────
    2 □ 2 1 9
```

6)
```
    1 □ 1 0 1
  + 2 2 5 4 □
  ─────────────
    3 2 □ 4 4
```

7)
```
    1 1 4 4 □
  + 1 □ 2 5 9
  ─────────────
    2 7 6 □ 9
```

8)
```
    1 0 □ 8 9
  +   8 1 1 □
  ─────────────
    1 □ 1 0 1
```

9)
```
    8 □ 3 3
  +   5 4 0 □
  ─────────────
    1 □ 0 4 2
```

10)
```
    □ 7 6 7
  + 1 0 6 0 □
  ─────────────
    2 0 □ 6 9
```

11)
```
    1 □ 0 8 6
  +   4 3 2 □
  ─────────────
    1 4 □ 1 4
```

12)
```
    9 8 □ 3
  + 1 □ 0 3 4
  ─────────────
    2 8 □ 6 7
```

13)
```
    1 0 □ 6 0
  + 1 9 3 8 □
  ─────────────
    □ 0 0 4 5
```

14)
```
    1 0 3 6 □
  + 1 0 □ 3 3
  ─────────────
    2 0 3 □ 3
```

15)
```
    1 0 9 1 □
  + 1 □ 9 7 1
  ─────────────
    2 6 □ 8 6
```

16)
```
    1 □ 0 5 5
  +   6 □ 5 0
  ─────────────
    1 6 3 0 □
```

17)
```
    1 1 4 2 □
  + 1 6 □ 0 6
  ─────────────
    2 □ 7 2 8
```

18)
```
    □ 9 8 1
  + 1 0 0 2 □
  ─────────────
    2 0 □ 0 1
```

Score / Date: _____

Fill in the missing digits.

1)
```
  1 1 4 2 ☐
+   2 0 9 ☐ 6
─────────────
  3 ☐ 3 5 7
```

2)
```
    8 4 6 ☐
+ 1 ☐ 7 7 8
─────────────
  1 9 2 ☐ 0
```

3)
```
  1 1 1 ☐ 8
+ 1 ☐ 6 2 3
─────────────
  2 6 8 1 ☐
```

4)
```
    9 1 6 ☐
+   9 ☐ 3 8
─────────────
  1 ☐ 3 0 0
```

5)
```
  1 0 8 7 ☐
+ 1 ☐ 3 7 0
─────────────
  2 6 2 ☐ 6
```

6)
```
  1 ☐ 1 6 3
+ 1 5 7 0 ☐
─────────────
  2 5 ☐ 6 5
```

7)
```
    8 9 6 ☐
+   5 4 ☐ 8
─────────────
  1 ☐ 3 8 1
```

8)
```
  1 0 5 ☐ 3
+ 1 ☐ 7 8 5
─────────────
  2 7 ☐ 5 8
```

9)
```
    8 6 ☐ 4
+ 1 ☐ 8 3 0
─────────────
  2 6 5 2 ☐
```

10)
```
  1 0 ☐ 4 4
+   7 1 8 ☐
─────────────
  1 8 0 ☐ 6
```

11)
```
    8 ☐ 7 1
+   5 7 3 ☐
─────────────
  1 ☐ 1 0 5
```

12)
```
  ☐ 2 7 7
+ 1 2 8 6 ☐
─────────────
  2 2 ☐ 3 7
```

13)
```
  1 1 ☐ 6 1
+ 1 8 9 5 ☐
─────────────
  3 ☐ 0 1 3
```

14)
```
    9 ☐ 1 8
+ 1 4 8 3 ☐
─────────────
  2 ☐ 6 5 1
```

15)
```
  1 0 ☐ 0 8
+   5 1 4 ☐
─────────────
  1 ☐ 0 5 0
```

16)
```
    8 ☐ 9 1
+ 2 0 7 8 ☐
─────────────
  2 9 3 ☐ 6
```

17)
```
  ☐ 1 2 0
+ 1 9 3 6 ☐
─────────────
  2 8 ☐ 8 9
```

18)
```
  1 1 3 6 ☐
+   5 ☐ 6 2
─────────────
  1 ☐ 2 2 6
```

Finding Digits In Subtractions

Ones	15–9=6	5 is smaller than 9. Combine 2 place values i.e. hundreds and tens. Regroup 80 tens to 79 tens 10 ones. 10 ones + 5 ones = 15 ones
Tens	9–□=3	79 tens = 7 hundreds 9 tens. Missing digit is 6
Hundreds	7–2=5	
Thousands	□–4=7	7+4=11. Regroup 5 ten thousands to 4 ten thousands 10 thousands. 11 ten thousands = 10 thousands + 1 thousand. With the regrouping, missing digit is 1.
Ten Thousands	4–0=□	Missing digit is 4.

$$\begin{array}{r} \overset{4}{5}\,\boxed{1}\,\overset{7\;9}{8\,0}\,\overset{1}{5} \\ -\quad 4\,2\,\boxed{6}\,9 \\ \hline \boxed{4}\,7\,5\,3\,6 \end{array}$$

Fill in the missing digits.

1)
$$\begin{array}{r} 5\,2\,\boxed{}\,1 \\ -\ 2\,\boxed{}\,8\,3 \\ \hline 2\,6\,9\,8 \end{array}$$

2)
$$\begin{array}{r} 5\,\boxed{}\,1\,1 \\ -\ 4\,0\,7\,\boxed{} \\ \hline 1\,6\,3\,4 \end{array}$$

3)
$$\begin{array}{r} \boxed{}\,3\,6\,3 \\ -\ 2\,7\,\boxed{}\,4 \\ \hline 1\,5\,6\,9 \end{array}$$

4)
$$\begin{array}{r} 2\,6\,\boxed{}\,3 \\ -\ \boxed{}\,0\,8\,0 \\ \hline 1\,5\,4\,3 \end{array}$$

5)
$$\begin{array}{r} \boxed{}\,9\,4\,\boxed{} \\ -\ 4\,0\,0\,2 \\ \hline 2\,9\,3\,9 \end{array}$$

6)
$$\begin{array}{r} 5\,\boxed{}\,6\,7 \\ -\ 3\,2\,0\,\boxed{} \\ \hline 1\,9\,6\,5 \end{array}$$

7)
$$\begin{array}{r} 6\,\boxed{}\,7\,9 \\ -\ 2\,1\,8\,\boxed{} \\ \hline 4\,5\,9\,9 \end{array}$$

8)
$$\begin{array}{r} \boxed{}\,9\,0\,4 \\ -\ 2\,9\,\boxed{}\,9 \\ \hline 3\,9\,0\,5 \end{array}$$

9)
$$\begin{array}{r} 4\,1\,5\,\boxed{} \\ -\ \boxed{}\,4\,0\,4 \\ \hline 2\,7\,5\,1 \end{array}$$

10)
$$\begin{array}{r} 6\,\boxed{}\,1\,7 \\ -\ 4\,7\,7\,\boxed{} \\ \hline 1\,8\,4\,5 \end{array}$$

11)
$$\begin{array}{r} 7\,4\,0\,\boxed{} \\ -\ 4\,\boxed{}\,1\,3 \\ \hline 3\,2\,9\,5 \end{array}$$

12)
$$\begin{array}{r} 7\,3\,\boxed{}\,6 \\ -\ 3\,\boxed{}\,4\,9 \\ \hline 3\,6\,1\,7 \end{array}$$

Score /   Date: _____

Fill in the missing digits.

1) 6 □ 2 0 6
  − 4 1 □ 4 0
  ──────────
    2 4 1 6 □

2) 4 7 8 2 □
  − 2 □ 0 3 8
  ──────────
    2 7 □ 8 9

3) 6 □ 8 5 2
  − 5 0 0 9 □
  ──────────
    1 8 □ 6 2

4) 6 □ 7 7 1
  − 4 3 □ 9 1
  ──────────
    2 4 5 8 □

5) 3 □ 0 5 4
  − 2 9 0 □ 1
  ──────────
    7 □ 6 3

6) 6 □ 3 6 8
  − 2 0 1 9 □
  ──────────
  □ 1 1 7 4

7) 7 4 □ 8 9
  − 1 8 7 5 □
  ──────────
    5 □ 5 3 2

8) 3 □ 4 □ 1
  − 1 3 7 5 □
  ──────────
    2 0 □ 9 0

9) 2 6 2 □ 9
  − 2 □ 4 9 9
  ──────────
    1 7 5 □

10) 3 □ 0 7 8
   − 2 0 9 4 □
   ──────────
     1 8 □ 3 4

11) 4 9 1 □ 2
   − 1 □ 7 6 7
   ──────────
     3 6 □ 5 5

12) 4 7 9 1 □
   − 2 □ 6 9 4
   ──────────
     2 2 □ 1 9

13) 2 3 □ 5 3
   − 2 0 3 7 □
   ──────────
   □ 4 7 6

14) 6 6 3 7 □
   − 1 □ 9 2 8
   ──────────
     5 3 □ 4 7

15) 1 □ 5 7 1
   − 1 3 □ 2 5
   ──────────
     5 8 4 □

16) 3 4 0 9 □
   − 1 9 1 □ 9
   ──────────
     1 □ 9 0 1

17) 6 □ 9 9 9
   − 4 6 □ 2 5
   ──────────
     1 5 4 7 □

18) □ 3 3 6 3
   − 2 5 0 □ 2
   ──────────
     2 8 □ 9 1

Fill in the missing digits.

1)
```
    5 1 3 □ 8
  -   3 □ 5 7 0
  ─────────────
    1 8 7 9 □
```

2)
```
    4 8 5 9 □
  - 4 □ 8 4 4
  ───────────
      3 □ 5 4
```

3)
```
    6 0 0 5 □
  - 1 0 □ 7 8
  ───────────
    □ 9 5 7 3
```

4)
```
    2 2 8 □ 3
  - 1 □ 0 5 8
  ───────────
    1 1 □ 8 5
```

5)
```
    7 □ 6 8 0
  - 1 3 7 7 □
  ───────────
    5 8 9 □ 9
```

6)
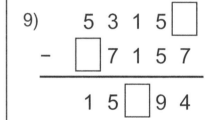
```
    □ 5 7 2 5
  - 4 7 □ 4 5
  ───────────
      8 5 □ 0
```

7)
```
    4 8 □ 8 2
  - 3 0 9 7 □
  ───────────
    1 □ 7 0 9
```

8)
```
    4 9 □ 2 8
  - 3 □ 8 3 2
  ───────────
    1 4 6 □ 6
```

9)
```
    5 3 1 5 □
  - □ 7 1 5 7
  ───────────
    1 5 □ 9 4
```

10)
```
    4 4 6 9 □
  - 1 □ 9 4 9
  ───────────
    3 3 7 □ 0
```

11)
```
    5 0 7 3 □
  - 3 □ 7 3 2
  ───────────
    1 5 □ 9 8
```

12)
```
    5 6 □ 8 3
  - 1 7 8 7 □
  ───────────
    3 □ 7 1 2
```

13)
```
    □ 1 0 7 8
  - 1 □ 8 8 8
  ───────────
    3 2 1 □ 0
```

14)
```
    4 □ 5 7 6
  - 2 8 □ 0 8
  ───────────
    2 1 1 □ 8
```

15)
```
    5 1 5 □ 7
  - □ 1 0 7 6
  ───────────
    3 0 □ 6 1
```

16)
```
    5 9 6 □ 9
  - 1 □ 0 5 6
  ───────────
    □ 1 6 1 3
```

17)
```
    7 3 0 □ 8
  - □ 8 6 7 6
  ───────────
    3 4 □ 1 2
```

18)
```
    2 □ 1 4 6
  - 1 9 3 □ 2
  ───────────
      4 □ 4 4
```

Score ___/___   Date: _____

Fill in the missing digits.

1)
```
    4 1 1 □ 3
  -   3 □ 3 3 2
  ───────────
      2 □ 5 1
```

2)
```
    4 8 2 6 □
  -   3 2 □ 3 1
  ───────────
      1 □ 0 3 8
```

3)
```
    4 □ 0 5 4
  -   1 7 5 2 □
  ───────────
      2 3 □ 3 4
```

4)
```
    7 2 0 4 □
  -   4 □ 2 1 5
  ───────────
      2 7 8 □ 4
```

5)
```
    □ 2 9 0 1
  -   1 0 4 □ 7
  ───────────
      6 2 □ 2 4
```

6)
```
    2 □ 3 7 1
  -   2 4 □ 0 9
  ───────────
        2 2 □ 2
```

7)
```
    5 1 □ 8 0
  -   1 0 6 3 □
  ───────────
      □ 0 8 4 3
```

8)
```
    □ 5 0 8 0
  -   1 6 2 □ 9
  ───────────
      1 □ 7 9 1
```

9)
```
    7 3 2 □ 8
  -   1 4 □ 0 4
  ───────────
      5 8 7 6 □
```

10)
```
    5 9 9 □ 8
  -   4 □ 1 7 3
  ───────────
      1 4 □ 1 5
```

11)
```
    3 9 4 □ 2
  -   3 □ 9 2 2
  ───────────
      7 □ 0 0
```

12)
```
    7 4 4 □ 5
  -   2 □ 0 5 0
  ───────────
      □ 0 4 4 5
```

13)
```
    6 □ 8 0 3
  -   2 4 8 3 □
  ───────────
      3 6 9 □ 4
```

14)
```
    6 9 7 1 □
  -   2 5 9 □ 0
  ───────────
      4 □ 7 4 9
```

15)
```
    6 7 4 □ 3
  -   □ 5 3 6 6
  ───────────
      3 □ 1 1 7
```

16)
```
    4 □ 4 8 8
  -   1 3 1 □ 7
  ───────────
      3 0 □ 2 1
```

17)
```
    2 □ 1 1 8
  -   1 6 7 □ 5
  ───────────
      7 □ 3 3
```

18)
```
    5 □ 9 1 2
  -   1 2 0 3 □
  ───────────
      4 6 □ 7 8
```

Please scan below and leave your review.

Answers

Page 2:
(1) 1,724 (2) 2,359 (3) 2,137 (4) 4,083

Page 3:
(1) 3,503 (2) 2,247 (3) 4,130 (4) 2,372

Page 4:
(1) 5,009 (2) 1,360 (3) 2,197 (4) 378

Page 5:
(1) 3,224 (2) 759 (3) 2,076 (4) 1,540

Page 8:

		Hundred Thousands	Ten Thousands	Thousands	Hundreds	Tens	Ones
1)	146,309	1	4	6	3	0	9
2)	27,820		2	7	8	2	0
3)	6,124			6	1	2	4
4)	53,476		5	3	4	7	6
5)	231				2	3	1
6)	122,917	1	2	2	9	1	7
7)	495,234	4	9	5	2	3	4
8)	76,085		7	6	0	8	5
9)	321,498	3	2	1	4	9	8
10)	14,372		1	4	3	7	2

Page 9:
(1) 100,000+40,000+6,000+300+9 (2) 20,000+7,000+800+20 (3) 6,000+100+20+4 (4) 50,000+3,000+400+70+6 (5) 200+30+1 (6) 100,000+20,000+2,000+900+10+7 (7) 400,000+90,000+5,000+200+30+4 (8) 70,000+6,000+80+5 (9) 300,000+20,000+1,000+400+90+8 (10)10,000+4,000+300+70+2

Page 10:

1)	712,897	7	1	2	8	9	7
2)	30,204		3	0	2	0	4
3)	2,560			2	5	6	0
4)	843,629	8	4	3	6	2	7
5)	48,715		4	8	7	1	5
6)	942				9	4	2

Page 10:

		Hundred Thousands	Ten Thousands	Thousands	Hundreds	Tens	Ones
7)	6,298			6	2	9	8
8)	523,624	5	2	3	6	2	4
9)	69,132		6	9	1	3	2
10)	951,487	9	5	1	4	8	7

Page 11:

700,000+10,000+2,000+800+90+7 (2) 30,000+200+4 (3) 2,000+500+60 (4) 800,000+40,000+3,000 +600+20+9 (5) 40,000+8,000+700+10+5 (6) 900+40+2 (7) 6,000+200+90+8 (8)500,000+20,000+3,000 +600+20+4 (9) 60,000+9,000+100+30+2 (10) 900,000+50,000+1,000+400+80+7

Page 12:

1)	852				8	5	2
2)	671,432	6	7	1	4	3	2
3)	30,876		3	0	8	7	6
4)	274,980	2	7	4	9	8	0
5)	72,681		7	2	6	8	1
6)	9,234			9	2	3	4
7)	378				3	7	8
8)	236,912	2	3	6	9	1	2
9)	432,689	4	3	2	6	8	9
10)	645,001	6	4	5	0	0	1

Page 13:

(1) 800+50+2 (2) 600,000+70,000+1,000+400+30+2 (3) 30,000+800+70+6 (4) 200,000+ 70,000+4,000 +900+80 (5) 70,000+2,000+600+80+1 (6) 9,000+200+30+4 (7) 300+70+8 (8) 200,000+30,000+6,000+ 900+10+2 (9) 400,000+30,000+2,000+600+80+9 (10) 600,000 +40,000+5,000+1

Page 14:

1)	81,930		8	1	9	3	0
2)	935				9	3	5
3)	241,009	2	4	1	0	0	9
4)	6,827			6	8	2	7
5)	78,033		7	8	0	3	3
6)	104,058	1	0	4	0	5	8
7)	63,981		6	3	9	8	1

Page 14:

		Hundred Thousands	Ten Thousands	Thousands	Hundreds	Tens	Ones
8)	690				6	9	0
9)	500,834	5	0	0	8	3	4
10)	1,008			1	0	0	8

Page 15:
(1) 80,000+1,000+900+30 (2) 900+30+5 (3) 200,000+40,000+1,000+9 (4) 6,000+800+20 +7 (5) 70,000 +8,000+30+3 (6) 100,000+4,000+50+8 (7) 60,000+3,000+900+80+1 (8) 600+90 (9) 500,000+800+30+4 (10) 1,000+8

Page 16:
(1) 4,000 (2) 40 (3) 400,000 (4) 400 (5) 4 (6) 100 (7) 10,000 (8) 1,000 (9) 10 (10) 100,000 (11) 7 (2) (12) 7,000 (13) 70 (14) 700,000 (15) 70,000

Page 17:
(1) 90 (2) 90,000 (3) 900 (4) 9,000 (5) 900,000 (6) 800 (7) 8,000 (8) 8 (9) 800,000 (10) 80 (11) 20,000 (12) 200,000 (13) 2,000 (14) 2 (15) 200

Page 18:
(1) 50 (2) 5,000 (3) 500,000 (4) 500 (5) 50,000 (6) 300,000 (7) 30 (8) 3,000 (9) 3 (10) 300 (11) 60,000 (12) 600 (13) 60 (14) 600,000 (15) 6,000

Page 19:
(1) 900 (2) 9 (3) 900,000 (4) 9,000 (5) 90,000 (6) 4,000 (7) 40,000 (8) 400 (9) 400,000 (10) 40 (11) 700,000 (12) 700 (13) 70,000 (14) 70 (15) 7,000

Page 20:
(1) 852,379 (2) 90 (3) 900 (4) 0 (5) 60 (6) 300,000 (7) 200,000 (8) 45,684 (9) 6,000 (10) 900 (11) 20,000 (12) 3,000 (13) 207,560 (14) 50 (15) 400

Page 21:
(1) 230,468 (2) 60,000 (3) 748,235 (4) 3,000 (5) 70,000 (6) 200,721 (7) 0 (8) 700 (9) 6,000 (10) 500,000 (11) 481,403 (12) 200,000 (13) 20,000 (14) 200 (15) 16,730

Page 22:
(1) 6,000 (2) 9,000 (3) 400,000 (4) 220,389 (5) 20,000 (6) 400,000 (7) 100,000 (8) 53,420 (9) 3,000 (10) 400,000 (11) 58,003 (12) 50,000 (13) 3,000 (14) 2,000 (15) 800,000

Page 23:
(1) 35,712 (2) 256,272 (3) 49,631 (4) 761,255 (5) 329,256 (6) 313,900 (7) 511,208 (8) 23,731 (9) 430,962 (10) 71,207 (11) 12,495 (12) 853 (13) 145,301 (14) 9,299 (15) 58,264

Page 24:
(1) 258,645 (2) 114,012 (3) 601,254 (4) 300,485 (5) 5,672 (6) 913,049 (7) 82,431 (8) 509,224 (9) 274,158 (10) 412,000 (11) 9,365 (12) 305,241 (13) 615,906 (14) 80,522 (15) 743,516

Page 25:
(1) 26,468 (2) 905,089 (3) 64,712 (4) 345,203 (5) 500,261 (6) 816,192 (7) 607,540 (8) 290,408 (9) 36,359 (10) 835,216 (11) 27,923 (12) 91,246 (13) 11,350 (14) 243,007 (15) 5,391

Page 26:
(1) 418,302 (2) 250,611 (3) 761,475 (4) 100,082 (5) 98,431 (6) 7,215 (7) 420,399 (8) 302,108 (9) 12,463 (10) 118,192 (11) 5,225 (12) 174,362 (13) 95,328 (14) 631,280 (15) 409,039

Page 27:
(1) Five hundred thirty-one thousand, nine hundred twelve (2) Two hundred fifty-nine thousand, seven hundred twenty (3) Eighty-six thousand, six hundred seventy-four (4) Nine thousand, six hundred three (5) Fourteen thousand, eight hundred twenty-seven (6) Six hundred thirty thousand, sixty-seven (7) Four hundred eighty-six thousand, one hundred seventy-five (8) Five thousand, six hundred nine (9) Three hundred seventy-five thousand, five (10) Eight hundred four thousand, three hundred (11) Twenty-seven thousand, ninety-five (12) Six thousand, three hundred twenty

Page 28:
(1) Seventy-three thousand, seven hundred sixty-five (2) Two thousand, six hundred ninety-five (3) Nine hundred thousand, one hundred twenty-seven (4) Eighteen thousand, nine hundred fifty-six (5) Three hundred fifty (6) Three hundred forty-nine thousand, two hundred thirty-five (7) Fifty-eight thousand, seven (8) Two hundred thirty-seven thousand, four hundred eighty-five (9) One hundred nine thousand, thirty-three (10) Two thousand, one hundred fifty-six (11) Eighty-six thousand, five hundred seventy-nine (12) Nine hundred twenty-five thousand, eight hundred thirty-four

Page 29:
(1) Three thousand, eight hundred two (2) Eighty-three thousand, three hundred eighty-nine (3) Five hundred ninety thousand, one hundred fifty-three (4) Six hunred thousand, three hundred forty-six (5) Twenty-seven thousand, one hundred five (6) Two hundred thirty thousand, four hundred (7) Seven hundred eighty-nine thousand, thirty-four (8) One hundred seventy-two thousand, nine hundred eighty-two (9) Nine houndred seven thousand, two hundred thirty-four (10) Five hundred thirty-three (11) Eighty-one thousand, two hundred ninety (12) Four hundred fifteen thousand, eleven

Page 30:
(1) Seventy-six thousand, nine hundred eighty-two (2) One hundred three thousand, nine hundred eighty-three (3) Fifty-one thousand, eight (4) Four hundred thirty-one (5) Fifty-eight thousand, nine hundred ninety-two (6) Four hundred eighteen thousand, nine hundred (7) Two hundred eighty-three thousand, four hundred eighty-eight (8) Sixty-seven thousand, ninety-three (9) Two thousand, seven hundred eighty-two (10) One hundred twenty thousand (11) Eighty-three thousand, three hundred twenty (12) Seven hundred thirty-nine

Page 31:
(1) 256,078; Two hundred fifty-six thousand, seventy-eight (2) Sixty-one thousand, seven hundred eighty-five; 60,000+1,000+700+80+5 (3) 437,629; 400,000+30,000+7,000+600+20+9 (4) 98,757; 90,000+8,000+700+50+7 (5) 886,927; Eight hundred eighty-six thousand, nine hundred twenty-seven

Page 32:
(1) 70,935; 70,000+900+30+5 (2) 851,732; Eight hundred fifty-one, seven hundred thirty-two (3) 538,205; 500,000+30,000+8,000+200+5 (4) Ninety-five thousand, three hundred ninety-two; 90,000+5,000+300+90+2 (5) 740,368; Seven hundred forty, three hundred sixty-eight

Page 33:
(1) 251,812; 200,000+50,000+1,000+800+10+2 (2) One hunderd thirty-three, six hundred ninety; 100,000+30,000+3,000+600+90 (3) 685,932; 600,000+80,000+5,000+900+30+2 (4) 46,539; Forty-six thousand, five hundred thirty-nine (5) Three hundred six thousand, five hundred sixty; 300,000+6,000+500+60

Page 36:
(1) 124,762; 10; 93,425 (2) 6,291; 10; 837,605 (3) 25,002; 100; 682,354 (4) 8,403; 100; 591,083 (5) 461,735; 100; 920,316 (6) 236,804; 10; 503,721

Page 37:
(1) 60,934; 10; 576,204 (2) 91,475; 10; 741 (3) 98,957; 10; 421,893 (4) 97,623; 100; 293,671 (5) 57,249; 100; 183,592 (6) 236,804; 10; 403,271

Page 38:
(1) 193,732; 10; 86,574 (2) 183,004; 10; 295,371 (3) 52,734; 1,000; 8,632 (4) 125, 867; 10; 733,598 (5) 928,645; 100; 49,627 (6) 193,224; 100; 72,930

Page 39:
(1) b (2) b (3) a (4) a (5) c (6) c (7) b (8) c

Page 40:
(1) b (2) c (3) b (4) a (5) b (6) b (7) b (8) b

Page 41:
(1) c (2) b (3) c (4) c (5) b (6) c (7) a (8) b

Page 42:
(1) > (2) > (3) < (4) < (5) < (6) < (7) < (8) > (9) < (10) < (11) < (12) > (13) > (14) >

Page 43:
(1) > (2) > (3) > (4) < (5) < (6) < (7) > (8) > (9) < (10) < (11) < (12) > (13) > (14) < (15) > (16) < (17) < (18) > (19) > (20) > (21) < (22) < (23) < (24) <

Page 44:
(1) < (2) < (3) < (4) > (5) > (6) < (7) < (8) > (9) > (10) < (11) > (12) > (13) < (14) > (15) < (16) > (17) > (18) < (19) > (20) < (21) > (22) > (23) < (24) >

Page 45:
(1) > (2) < (3) < (4) < (5) > (6) < (7) < (8) < (9) > (10) > (11) < (12) < (13) > (14) < (15) > (16) < (17) < (18) < (19) < (20) > (21) > (22) > (23) < (24) >

Page 46:
(1) 679,832 (2) 8,902 (3) 134,789 (4) 97,098 (5) 7,991 (6) 181 (7) 52,091 (8) 27,891 (9) 3,506 (10) 82,750 (11) 97,200 (12) 4,726

Page 47:
(1) 2,931 (2) 689 (3) 7,001 (4) 812,524 (5) 3,089 (6) 50,302 (7) 1,098 (8) 20,395 (9) 284 (10) 9,012 (11) 415,780 (12) 30,098

Page 48:
(1) 792 (2) 48,102 (3) 562,008 (4) 99,059 (5) 3,452 (6) 296,782 (7) 6,921 (8) 4,503 (9) 8,520 (10) 1,872 (11) 70,026 (12) 547,034

Page 50:
(1) 5,062; 50,286; 56,782; 59,087 (2) 12,981; 21,871; 102,809; 120,712 (3) 3,061; 3,156; 3,561; 3,665

Page 51:
(1) 6,923; 64,321; 65,872; 75,892 (2) 123,609; 137,870; 210,673; 218,954 (3) 80,239; 82,145; 88,102; 89,672 (4) 12,004; 12,426; 13,047; 13,843 (5) 4,023; 4,834; 4,902; 40,812 (6) 33,502; 306,156; 313,934; 331,613 (7) 8,348; 46,234; 48,923; 84,283 (8) 7,012; 7,264; 7,462; 7,894

Page 52:
(1) 5,805; 5,891; 50,832; 55,123 (2) 92,903; 93,001; 96,734; 98,672 (3) 405,127; 423,817; 432,083; 488,263 (4) 2,061; 2,893; 20,176; 21,527 (5) 605,202; 614,729; 630,281; 672,051 (6) 4,276; 35,903; 38,319; 43,732 (7) 122,034; 125,723; 126,741; 129,683 (8) 10,450; 14,065; 14,560; 14,658

Page 53:
(1) 235,972; 235,961; 235,182; 235,026 (2) 7,812; 7,481; 7,418; 7,408 (3) 985; 958; 955; 908 (4) 69,712; 62,392; 61,751; 60,302 (5) 47,298; 40,581; 4,918; 4,073 (6) 76,403; 74,062; 73,640; 70,621 (7) 654,032; 650,324; 623,056; 600,562 (8) 1,308; 1,180; 1,003; 183

Page 54:
(1) 91,451; 90,783; 19,761; 9,304 (2) 169,712; 166,048; 164,408; 160,712 (3) 739,236; 738,028; 733,004; 732,009 (4) 40,009; 4,903; 4,300; 4,093 (5) 59,032; 57,628; 56,216; 51,043 (6) 89,381; 86,003; 84,512; 81,078 (7) 374,192; 371,645; 370,682; 307,526 (8) 8,930; 8,903; 8,093; 893

Page 55:
(1)(a) 6,530 (b) 3,056 (2)(a) 8,632 (b) 2,368 (3)(a) 9,410 (b) 1,049

Page 56:
(1)(a) 4,301 (b) 1,034 (2)(a) 6,532 (b) 2,356 (3)(a) 8,420 (b) 2,048 (4)(a) 9,421 (b) 1,249 (5)(a) 8,750 (b) 5,078

Page 57:
(1)(a) 87,520 (b) 20,578 (2)(a) 98,642 (b) 24,689 (3)(a) 84,210 (b) 10,248 (4)(a) 94,321 (b) 12,349 (5)(a) 75,430 (b) 30,457

Page 58:
(1)(a) 976,432 (b) 234,679 (2)(a) 854,210 (b) 102,458 (3)(a) 763,210 (b) 102,367 (4)(a) 754,320 (b) 203,457 (5)(a) 975,321 (b) 123,579

Page 59:
(1) 420; 720 (2) 13,436; 13,446 (3) 3,372; 4,372; 7,372 (4) 5,144; 5,146; 5,147 (5) 41,273; 41,573; 41,773 (6) 21,421; 31,421; 61,421 (7) 74,910; 74,940; 74,960 (8) 9,271; 9,272; 9,275 (9) 25,156; 27,156; 28,156 (10) 12,209; 12,509; 12,709

Page 60:
(1) 1,260; 1,280 (2) 6,220; 6,520 (3) 40,844; 40,864; 40,874 (4) 9,353; 9,356; 9,368 (5) 12,283; 15,283 (6) 527; 827 (7) 82,045; 85,045; 87,045 (8) 37,138; 37,158 (9) 30,921; 40,921; 50,921 (10) 3,196; 5,196; 7,196

Page 61:
(1) 550; 530 (2) 21,889; 21,589 (3) 4,979; 4,977; 4,974 (4) 72,500; 42,500; 22,500 (5) 7,378; 7,368 (6) 31,531; 28,531; 26,531 (7) 857; 827 (8) 9,910; 9,710; 9,410 (9) 50,879; 50,877; 50,876 (10) 2,472; 2,462; 2,432

Page 62:
(1) 6,721; 6,741; 6,761 (2) 983; 953 (3) 28,485; 26,485; 23,485 (4) 32,877; 32,874; 32,872 (5) 21,403; 22,403 (6) 8,220; 8,250; 8,270 (7) 389; 689 (8) 3,159; 3,157; 3,154 (9) 57,201; 55,201; 54,201; (10) 7,300; 7,400; 7,700

Page 64:
(1) ten thousands, thousands; thousands; thousands; hundreds; hundreds; tens; ones (2) ten thousands; ten thousands; thousands; thousands; hundreds; hundreds

Page 65:
(1) thousands, tens; thousands, tens, tens; thousands, tens; hundreds, tens; tens, tens; tens (2) thousands; hundreds; hundreds (3) hundred thousands; thousands; hundreds
(4) thousands, tens; hundreds, tens; tens, ten; tens

Page 66:
(1) thousands, tens; hundreds, tens, tens; hundreds, tens; hundreds, tens; hundreds, tens (2) thousands; hundreds; hundreds (3) thousands; thousands; hundreds; hundreds (4) thousands, tens; hundreds, tens; tens, tens; tens

Page 67:
(1) thousands, hundreds, tens; hundreds, hundreds, ones; hundreds, ones; tens, ones; tens, ones; tens, ones (2) hundreds, tens, ones; hundreds, ones; hundreds, tens, ones; hundreds, ones, ones; hundreds, ones (3) thousands, hundreds, ones; thousands, hundreds, ones; thousands, hundreds, tens, ones; thousands, hundreds, ones (4) hundreds, tens, ones; hundreds, tens, ones; hundreds, ones, ones; hundreds, ones

Page 68:
(1) 78 (2) 54,093 (3) 6,200 (4) 397 (5) 340 (6) 458, 9 (7) 80,000 (8) 36 (9) 2,568 (10) 795,608 (11) 93,837 (12) 8,000

Page 69:
(1) 10,538 (2) 430 (3) 87,652 (4) 689 (5) 55,407 (6) 945 (7) 6 (8) 93,786 (9) 654 (10) 32,182 (11) 800 (12) 280

Page 70:
(1) 642,734 (2) 87 (3) 8,700 (4) 15 (5) 345 (6) 8,305 (7) 3,759 (8) 1,649 (9) 589 (10) 540 (11) 78 (12) 3,427

Page 73:
(1) 570 (2) 90 (3) 4,160 (4) 130 (5) 34,850 (6) 217,850 (7) 70 (8) 539,670 (9) 4,800 (10) 129,500 (11) 700 (12) 41,000 (13) 800 (14) 12,700 (15) 385,800 (16) 900 (17) 36,000 (18) 132,000 (19) 282,000 (20) 700,000 (21) 5,000 (22) 440,000 (23) 693,000 (24) 8,000

Page 74:
(1) 8,100 (2) 75,700 (3) 30,800 (4) 98,300 (5) 23,100 (6) 1,000 (7) 500 (8) 70,600 (9) 315,000 (10) 61,000 (11) 58,000 (12) 194,000 (13) 73,000 (14) 833,000 (15) 2,000 (16) 244,000 (17) 90,000 (18) 490,000 (19) 240,000 (20) 60,000 (21) 810,000 (22) 30,000 (23) 10,000 (24) 860,000

Page 75:
(1) 4,000 (2) 12,000 (3) 359,000 (4) 91,000 (5) 816,000 (6) 5,000 (7) 703,000 (8) 22,000 (9) 280,000 (10) 60,000 (11) 30,000 (12) 840,000 (13) 200,000 (14) 30,000 (15) 80,000 (16) 90,000 (17) 800,000 (18) 300,000 (19) 800,000 (20) 100,000 (21) 900,000 (22) 700,000 (23) 500,000 (24) 400,000

Page 77:
(1) 588,200 (2) 686,143 (3) 547,892 (4) 483,065 (5) 286,613 (6) 508,180 (7) 422,489 (8) 827,912

Page 78:
(1) 532,609 (2) 421,513 (3) 767,494 (4) 629,666 (5) 551,607 (6) 680,049 (7) 361,994 (8) 301,095 (9) 296,639 (10) 369,431 (11) 308,484 (12) 407,894

Page 79:
(1) 529,687 (2) 279,622 (3) 603,919 (4) 409,486 (5) 484,565 (6) 522,638 (7) 640,830 (8) 502,981 (9) 693,946 (10) 711,341 (11) 427,685 (12) 700,071

Page 80:
(1) 246,353 (2) 408,356 (3) 433,607 (4) 477,316 (5) 518,191 (6) 614,513 (7) 210,920 (8) 473,251 (9) 565,670 (10) 568,889 (11) 466,897 (12) 811,938

Page 81:
(1) 321,714 (2) 515,614 (3) 595,117 (4) 299,134 (5) 487,322 (6) 652,925 (7) 451,640 (8) 529,023 (9) 556,718 (10) 390,726 (11) 803,471 (12) 364,728

Page 82:
(1) 508,388 (2) 583,047 (3) 382,025 (4) 340,099 (5) 370,897 (6) 475,611 (7) 401,925 (8) 561,965 (9) 483,599 (10) 333,102 (11) 465,282 (12) 365,170

Page 83:
(1) 532,256 (2) 253,972 (3) 578,406 (4) 366,746 (5) 463,888 (6) 513,906 (7) 266,985 (8) 240,800
(9) 666,320 (10) 559,967 (11) 477,123 (12) 612,719

Page 84:
(1) 167,172 (2) 725,816 (3) 502,733

Page 85:
(1) 419,060 (2) 361,921 (3) 629,189 (4) 601,807 (5) 638,185 (6) 594,043

Page 86:
(1) 548,815 (2) 479,324 (3) 486,138 (4) 622,867 (5) 703,040 (6) 418,489

Page 87:
(1) 421,513 (2) 629,666 (3) 680,049 (4) 301,095 (5) 369,431 (6) 407,894

Page 89:
(1) 284,606 (2) 67,907 (3) 53,890 (4) 349,922 (5) 297,490 (6) 430,106 (7) 311,961 (8) 452,457

Page 90:
(1) 137,836 (2) 314,979 (3) 301,001 (4) 210,100 (5) 189,454 (6) 67,463 (7) 211,406 (8) 350,223
(9) 369,548 (10) 582,109 (11) 151,606 (12) 282,652

Page 91:
(1) 247,570 (2) 398,772 (3) 93,613 (4) 310,119 (5) 421,159 (6) 189,435 (7) 401,188 (8) 291,746
(9) 116,687 (10) 171,447 (11) 328,247 (12) 108,077

Page 92:
(1) 43,214 (2) 537,602 (3) 503,625 (4) 123,929 (5) 123,290 (6) 80,438 (7) 79,988 (8) 61,824 (9) 318,724
(10) 330,157 (11) 127,582 (12) 246,664

Page 93:
(1)166,788 (2)180,890 (3) 372,84 (4) 269,597

Page 94:
(1) 286,258 (2) 137,456 (3) 151,968 (4) 414,758 (5) 286,326 (6) 461,738

Page 95:
(1) 92,922 (2) 491,823 (3) 444,241 (4) 537,789 (5) 262,981 (6)130,567

Page 97:
(1) 293,864 (2) 286,327 (3) 237,714 (4) 411,003 (5) 151,681 (6) 368,904 (7) 128,788 (8) 412,834
(9)179,538 (10) 419,462 (11) 305,121 (12) 154,496

Page 98:
(1) 7,755 (2) 258,697 (3) 159,796 (4) 163,797 (5) 35,298 (6) 295,992 (7) 254,786 (8) 211,615 (9)
179,960 (10) 168,653 (11) 216,750 (12) 162,360

Page 99:,
(1) 383,870 (2) 141,028 (3) 160,668 (4) 312,204 (5) 480,842 (6) 286,884 (7) 480,274 (8) 239,693
(9) 447,163 (10) 248,945 (11) 363,535 (12) 168,275

Page 100:
(1) 136,036 (2) 249,735 (3) 139,680 (4) 370,416 (5) 211,549 (6) 208,052 (7) 217,012 (8) 219,798
(9) 150,183 (10) 382,455 (11) 480,760 (12) 252,574

Page 102:
(1) 230,524 (2) 673,023 (3) 9,658 (4) 690,935 (5) 26,400 (6) 356,308 (7) 311,830 (8) 519,305 (9) 90,925
(10) 620,357 (11) 55,829 (12) 551,192

Page 103:

(1) 68,980 (2) 405,216 (3) 52,643 (4) 400,315 (5) 303,610 (6) 357,132 (7) 190,549
(8) 679,507 (9) 259,120 (10) 667,646 (11) 215,674 (12) 480,766

Page 104:

(1) 362,881 (2) 610,370 (3) 266,662 (4) 484,021 (5) 176,593 (6) 398,019 (7) 37,270
(8) 399,262 (9) 219,489 (10) 337,519 (11) 377,941 (12) 549,965

Page 105:

(1)
```
    4 0 3 [4]
  + 7 [9] 9 3
  ───────────
  1 2 0 2 7
```

(2)
```
    6 0 [9] 5
  + [5] 8 0 3
  ───────────
  1 1 8 9 8
```

(3)
```
    5 2 8 8
  + 2 [7] 3 [5]
  ───────────
    8 0 2 3
```

(4)
```
    5 [3] 9 [4]
  + 1 4 7 1
  ───────────
    6 8 6 5
```

(5)
```
    4 3 1 7
  + [6] 1 [4] 0
  ───────────
  1 0 4 5 7
```

(6)
```
    1 [7] 0 7
  + 2 7 3 [4]
  ───────────
    4 4 4 1
```

(7)
```
    2 0 [5] 4
  + [4] 7 1 0
  ───────────
    6 7 6 4
```

(8)
```
  [4] 4 7 [8]
  + 6 3 3 3
  ───────────
  1 0 8 1 1
```

(9)
```
    1 9 [8] 9
  + 1 [9] 9 2
  ───────────
    3 9 8 1
```

(10)
```
  [2] 0 4 [8]
  + 7 9 2 0
  ───────────
    9 9 6 8
```

(11)
```
    2 [6] 1 4
  + 6 3 5 [5]
  ───────────
    8 9 6 9
```

(12)
```
    3 2 4 [7]
  + [7] 6 6 6
  ───────────
  1 0 9 1 3
```

Page 106:

(1)
```
    1 0 8 [5] 9
  +     4 5 6 [8]
  ───────────────
  1 5 [4] 2 7
```

(2)
```
    1 0 9 [3] 6
  +   [7] 6 0 8
  ───────────────
  1 8 5 4 [4]
```

(3)
```
      9 [3] 8 9
  + 2 0 7 9 [8]
  ───────────────
  3 [0] 1 8 7
```

(4)
```
        9 8 [6] 9
  + 1 [5] 2 2 7
  ───────────────
  2 5 [0] 9 6
```

(5)
```
      [8] 5 1 2
  + 1 2 0 5 [9]
  ───────────────
  2 0 5 [7] 1
```

(6)
```
    1 [0] 5 8 1
  + 1 1 4 [8] 2
  ───────────────
  2 2 [0] 6 3
```

(7)
```
    1 [1] 1 1 7
  + 1 4 1 7 [9]
  ───────────────
  2 5 2 [9] 6
```

(8)
```
    1 0 [9] 3 7
  + 1 1 3 7 [5]
  ───────────────
  2 [2] 3 1 2
```

(9)
```
    1 1 9 7 [8]
  +     5 [8] 6 4
  ───────────────
  1 7 8 [4] 2
```

Page 106:

(10)
```
    8 9 0 2
+   2 2 1 4 4
-----------
  3 1 0 4 6
```

(11)
```
  1 1 7 8 3
+     4 2 4 5
-----------
  1 6 0 2 8
```

(12)
```
  1 1 4 3 5
+     6 7 6 5
-----------
  1 8 2 0 0
```

(13)
```
  1 0 1 5 4
+   1 4 5 7 9
-----------
  2 4 7 3 3
```

14)
```
  1 1 4 9 6
+   1 0 1 8 1
-----------
  2 1 6 7 7
```

(15)
```
      9 6 2 4
+     5 8 0 9
-----------
  1 5 4 3 3
```

(16)
```
  1 1 1 9 4
+   1 5 6 3 5
-----------
  2 6 8 2 9
```

(17)
```
      9 6 3 7
+   1 8 5 9 3
-----------
  2 8 2 3 0
```

(18)
```
      8 4 3 6
+   1 5 0 9 0
-----------
  2 3 5 2 6
```

Page 107:

(1)
```
  1 1 9 2 9
+   1 2 8 3 6
-----------
  2 4 7 6 5
```

(2)
```
      9 3 0 9
+   2 0 0 6 3
-----------
  2 9 3 7 2
```

(3)
```
      9 5 0 5
+   1 3 7 9 2
-----------
  2 3 2 9 7
```

(4)
```
      9 4 9 4
+   2 0 3 9 6
-----------
  2 9 8 9 0
```

(5)
```
      9 2 5 6
+   1 9 9 6 3
-----------
  2 9 2 1 9
```

(6)
```
  1 0 1 0 1
+   2 2 5 4 3
-----------
  3 2 6 4 4
```

(7)
```
  1 1 4 4 0
+   1 6 2 5 9
-----------
  2 7 6 9 9
```

(8)
```
  1 0 9 8 9
+     8 1 1 2
-----------
  1 9 1 0 1
```

(9)
```
      8 6 3 3
+     5 4 0 9
-----------
  1 4 0 4 2
```

(10)
```
      9 7 6 7
+   1 0 6 0 2
-----------
  2 0 3 6 9
```

(11)
```
  1 0 0 8 6
+     4 3 2 8
-----------
  1 4 4 1 4
```

(12)
```
      9 8 3 3
+   1 9 0 3 4
-----------
  2 8 8 6 7
```

(13)
```
  1 0 6 6 0
+   1 9 3 8 5
-----------
  3 0 0 4 5
```

14)
```
  1 0 3 6 0
+   1 0 0 3 3
-----------
  2 0 3 9 3
```

(15)
```
  1 0 9 1 5
+   1 5 9 7 1
-----------
  2 6 8 8 6
```

Page 107:

(16)
```
  1 0 0 5 5
+     6 2 5 0
-----------
  1 6 3 0 5
```

(17)
```
  1 1 4 2 2
+   1 6 3 0 6
-----------
  2 7 7 2 8
```

(18)
```
    9 9 8 1
+ 1 0 0 2 0
-----------
  2 0 0 0 1
```

Page 108:

(1)
```
  1 1 4 2 1
+ 2 0 9 3 6
-----------
  3 2 3 5 7
```

(2)
```
    8 4 6 2
+ 1 0 7 7 8
-----------
  1 9 2 4 0
```

(3)
```
  1 1 1 8 8
+ 1 5 6 2 3
-----------
  2 6 8 1 1
```

(4)
```
    9 1 6 2
+   9 1 3 8
-----------
  1 8 3 0 0
```

(5)
```
  1 0 8 7 6
+ 1 5 3 7 0
-----------
  2 6 2 4 6
```

(6)
```
  1 0 1 6 3
+ 1 5 7 0 2
-----------
  2 5 8 6 5
```

(7)
```
    8 9 6 3
+   5 4 1 8
-----------
  1 4 3 8 1
```

(8)
```
  1 0 5 7 3
+ 1 6 7 8 5
-----------
  2 7 3 5 8
```

(9)
```
    8 6 9 4
+ 1 7 8 3 0
-----------
  2 6 5 2 4
```

(10)
```
  1 0 8 4 4
+   7 1 8 2
-----------
  1 8 0 2 6
```

(11)
```
    8 3 7 1
+   5 7 3 4
-----------
  1 4 1 0 5
```

(12)
```
    9 2 7 7
+ 1 2 8 6 0
-----------
  2 2 1 3 7
```

(13)
```
  1 1 0 6 1
+ 1 8 9 5 2
-----------
  3 0 0 1 3
```

14)
```
    9 8 1 8
+ 1 4 8 3 3
-----------
  2 4 6 5 1
```

(15)
```
  1 0 9 0 8
+   5 1 4 2
-----------
  1 6 0 5 0
```

(16)
```
    8 5 9 1
+ 2 0 7 8 5
-----------
  2 9 3 7 6
```

(17)
```
    9 1 2 0
+ 1 9 3 6 9
-----------
  2 8 4 8 9
```

(18)
```
  1 1 3 6 4
+   5 8 6 2
-----------
  1 7 2 2 6
```

Page 109:

(1)
```
  5 2 8 1
- 2 5 8 3
---------
  2 6 9 8
```

(2)
```
  5 7 1 1
- 4 0 7 7
---------
  1 6 3 4
```

(3)
```
  4 3 6 3
- 2 7 9 4
---------
  1 5 6 9
```

Page 109:

(4)
```
  2 6 [2] 3
- [1] 0 8 0
-----------
  1 5 4 3
```

(5)
```
  [6] 9 4 [1]
-   4 0 0 2
-------------
    2 9 3 9
```

(6)
```
  5 [1] 6 7
- 3 2 0 [2]
-----------
  1 9 6 5
```

(7)
```
  6 [7] 7 9
- 2 1 8 [0]
-----------
  4 5 9 9
```

(8)
```
  [6] 9 0 4
- 2 9 [9] 9
-----------
  3 9 0 5
```

(9)
```
  4 1 5 [5]
- [1] 4 0 4
-----------
  2 7 5 1
```

(10)
```
  6 [6] 1 7
- 4 7 7 [2]
-----------
  1 8 4 5
```

(11)
```
  7 4 0 [8]
- 4 [1] 1 3
-----------
  3 2 9 5
```

(12)
```
  7 3 6 6
- 3 [7] 4 9
-----------
  3 6 1 7
```

Page 110:

(1)
```
  6 [5] 2 0 6
- 4 1 [0] 4 0
-------------
  2 4 1 6 [6]
```

(2)
```
  4 7 8 2 [7]
- 2 [0] 0 3 8
-------------
  2 7 [7] 8 9
```

(3)
```
  6 [8] 8 5 2
- 5 0 0 9 [0]
-------------
  1 8 [7] 6 2
```

(4)
```
  6 [7] 7 7 1
- 4 3 [1] 9 1
-------------
  2 4 5 8 [0]
```

(5)
```
  3 [7] 0 5 4
- 2 9 0 [9] 1
-------------
    7 [9] 6 3
```

(6)
```
  6 [1] 3 6 8
- 2 0 1 9 [4]
-------------
  [4] 1 1 7 4
```

(7)
```
  7 4 [2] 8 9
- 1 8 7 5 [7]
-------------
  5 [5] 5 3 2
```

(8)
```
  3 [4] 4 4 1
- 1 3 7 5 [1]
-------------
  2 0 [6] 9 0
```

(9)
```
  2 6 2 [4] 9
- 2 [4] 4 9 9
-------------
    1 7 5 [0]
```

(10)
```
  3 [9] 0 7 8
- 2 0 9 4 [4]
-------------
  1 8 [1] 3 4
```

(11)
```
  4 9 1 [2] 2
- 1 [2] 7 6 7
-------------
  3 6 [3] 5 5
```

(12)
```
  4 7 9 1 [3]
- 2 [5] 6 9 4
-------------
  2 2 [2] 1 9
```

(13)
```
  2 3 [8] 5 3
- 2 0 3 7 [7]
-------------
  [3] 4 7 6
```

14)
```
  6 6 3 7 [5]
- 1 [2] 9 2 8
-------------
  5 3 [4] 4 7
```

(15)
```
  1 [9] 5 7 1
- 1 3 [7] 2 5
-------------
    5 8 4 [6]
```

Page 110:

(16)
```
    3 4 0 9 [0]
  -   1 9 1 [8] 9
  ─────────────
    1 [4] 9 0 1
```

(17)
```
    6 [1] 9 9 9
  -   4 6 [5] 2 5
  ─────────────
    1 5 4 7 [4]
```

(18)
```
  [5] 3 3 6 3
  -   2 5 0 [7] 2
  ─────────────
    2 8 [2] 9 1
```

Page 111:

(1)
```
    5 1 3 [6] 8
  -   3 [2] 5 7 0
  ─────────────
    1 8 7 9 [8]
```

(2)
```
    4 8 5 9 [8]
  -   4 [4] 8 4 4
  ─────────────
      3 [7] 5 4
```

(3)
```
    6 0 0 5 [1]
  -   1 0 [4] 7 8
  ─────────────
  [4] 9 5 7 3
```

(4)
```
    2 2 8 [4] 3
  -   1 [1] 0 5 8
  ─────────────
    1 1 [7] 8 5
```

(5)
```
    7 [2] 6 8 0
  -   1 3 7 7 [1]
  ─────────────
    5 8 9 [0] 9
```

(6)
```
  [5] 5 7 2 5
  -   4 7 [1] 4 5
  ─────────────
      8 5 [8] 0
```

(7)
```
    4 8 [6] 8 2
  -   3 0 9 7 [3]
  ─────────────
    1 [7] 7 0 9
```

(8)
```
    4 9 [5] 2 8
  -   3 [4] 8 3 2
  ─────────────
    1 4 6 [9] 6
```

(9)
```
    5 3 1 5 [1]
  -   [3] 7 1 5 7
  ─────────────
    1 5 [9] 9 4
```

(10)
```
    4 4 6 9 [9]
  -   1 [0] 9 4 9
  ─────────────
    3 3 7 [5] 0
```

(11)
```
    5 0 7 3 [0]
  -   3 [4] 7 3 2
  ─────────────
    1 5 [9] 9 8
```

(12)
```
    5 6 [5] 8 3
  -   1 7 8 7 [1]
  ─────────────
    3 [8] 7 1 2
```

(13)
```
  [5] 1 0 7 8
  -   1 [8] 8 8 8
  ─────────────
    3 2 1 [9] 0
```

(14)
```
    4 [9] 5 7 6
  -   2 8 [4] 0 8
  ─────────────
    2 1 1 [6] 8
```

(15)
```
    5 1 5 [3] 7
  -   [2] 1 0 7 6
  ─────────────
    3 0 [4] 6 1
```

(16)
```
    5 9 6 [6] 9
  -   1 [8] 0 5 6
  ─────────────
  [4] 1 6 1 3
```

(17)
```
    7 3 0 [8] 8
  -   [3] 8 6 7 6
  ─────────────
    3 4 [4] 1 2
```

(18)
```
    2 [4] 1 4 6
  -   1 9 3 [0] 2
  ─────────────
      4 [8] 4 4
```

Page 112:

(1)
```
    4 1 1 [8] 3
  -   3 [8] 3 3 2
  ─────────────
      2 [8] 5 1
```

(2)
```
    4 8 2 6 [9]
  -   3 2 [2] 3 1
  ─────────────
    1 [6] 0 3 8
```

(3)
```
    4 [1] 0 5 4
  -   1 7 5 2 [0]
  ─────────────
    2 3 [5] 3 4
```

Page 112:

(4)
```
    7 2 0 4 [9]
  -   4 [4] 2 1 5
  ─────────────
    2 7 8 [3] 4
```

(5)
```
    [7] 2 9 0 1
  -   1 0 4 [7] 7
  ─────────────
    6 2 [4] 2 4
```

(6)
```
    2 [6] 3 7 1
  -   2 4 [1] 0 9
  ─────────────
      2 2 [6] 2
```

(7)
```
    5 1 [4] 8 0
  -   1 0 6 3 [7]
  ─────────────
    [4] 0 8 4 3
```

(8)
```
    [3] 5 0 8 0
  -   1 6 2 [8] 9
  ─────────────
    1 [8] 7 9 1
```

(9)
```
    7 3 2 [6] 8
  -   1 4 5 0 4
  ─────────────
    5 8 7 6 [4]
```

(10)
```
    5 9 9 [8] 8
  -   4 [5] 1 7 3
  ─────────────
    1 4 [8] 1 5
```

(11)
```
    3 9 4 [2] 2
  -   3 [1] 9 2 2
  ─────────────
      7 [5] 0 0
```

(12)
```
    7 4 4 [9] 5
  -   2 [4] 0 5 0
  ─────────────
    [5] 0 4 4 5
```

(13)
```
    6 [1] 8 0 3
  -   2 4 8 3 [9]
  ─────────────
    3 6 9 [6] 4
```

14)
```
    6 9 7 1 [9]
  -   2 5 9 [7] 0
  ─────────────
    4 [3] 7 4 9
```

(15)
```
    6 7 4 [8] 3
  -   [3] 5 3 6 6
  ─────────────
    3 [2] 1 1 7
```

(16)
```
    4 [3] 4 8 8
  -   1 3 1 [6] 7
  ─────────────
    3 0 [3] 2 1
```

(17)
```
    2 [4] 1 1 8
  -   1 6 7 [8] 5
  ─────────────
    7 [3] 3 3
```

(18)
```
    5 [8] 9 1 2
  -   1 2 0 3 [4]
  ─────────────
    4 6 [8] 7 8
```

Made in the USA
Las Vegas, NV
01 September 2024

94625284R00077